SUPREME

INFLUENCE

SUPREME
INFLUENCE

Change Your Life
with the
Power of the
Language
You Use

Niurka

HARMONY
BOOKS · NEW YORK

Illustration on page 52 by Kathy Klingaman; photograph on page 132
by Barry Selby and Kathy Klingaman

Library of Congress Cataloging-in-Publication Data
Niurka.
Supreme influence : change your life with the
power of the language you choose.
p. cm.
1. Neurolinguistics. 2. Brain—Localization of functions. I. Title.
QP399.N58 2013
612.8'2336—dc23
2012032517

ISBN 978-0-307-95687-3
eISBN 978-0-307-95689-7

Jacket design by Laura Duffy
Jacket illustrations © Shutterstock

1 3 5 7 9 10 8 6 4 2

FIRST EDITION

One person's awakening
elevates the consciousness
of the planet.
I am writing this book
for the One—
you.

Contents

SECTION III: EMPOWER

SECTION IV: EVOLVE

Author's Note

Welcome. Blessings. Love.

Dear One,

Magnificent synchronicity has brought us together at this sacred moment in eternity for a grand purpose, which will be revealed as we journey through these pages.

Individually and collectively, we stand at a perpetual crossroads, in a state of transition between what has been *and* what could be. *The choices we make—in thought, word, and action—create an immeasurable ripple effect, influencing everyone and everything around us. In any given instant, we are either choosing consciously (meaning we are aware of the effect of our decisions) or we are choosing unconsciously (that is, without awareness). Conscious choices affirm life; unaware choices destroy it. These choices are the seeds from which we shape our world. And here we are.*

You may be holding this book right now for the same reason that I wrote it: because we know . . . It is time. Now is the time to ascend to the next level, individually and collectively, so that we can consciously create a harmonious, prosperous, and sustainable future while honoring each one's uniqueness. We each have an important role to play. To live authentically, support others on their path, and fulfill our destiny, it is essential to elevate our thinking, evolve our language, and live with awareness of how our presence influences the whole of existence.

Allow me to share a bit about my life's work and what inspired me to write this book for you.

I'm passionate about guiding people to transform challenges and transcend limitations. Since I launched my company in 2000, I have taught and led tens of thousands of people to elevate the way they think, speak, and, ultimately, how they live. My live courses, retreats, and seminars are sacred spaces for conscious transformation where I guide people to release anything blocking them—mentally, emotionally, spiritually, and energetically.

At a young age, I knew my life's purpose and devoted myself to learning how to help people live genuinely, freely, and mightily.

My devotion led me to research and integrate wisdom from many realms—communication, cognitive neuroscience, psychology, quantum physics, spirituality, leadership, and business. My discoveries inspired the creation of Supreme Influence.

Working in Supreme Influence, and weaving in disciplines such as neuro-linguistic programming (the study of how language affects the nervous system), guided visualization, meditation, hypnosis, Time Line Therapy, pranic healing, as well as ancient wisdom traditions, I show my students how to integrate daily practices that activate their brilliance and naturally transform old habits, addictions, and/or repressed emotions such as anger, sadness, fear, guilt, or shame. My students have described their life as BSI (before Supreme Influence) and ASI (after Supreme Influence).

Many of the finest corporations in the world, including Mercedes-Benz, Prudential, and Marriott, have produced record-breaking results by applying my teachings. I've worked with people from all walks of life—CEOs of major corporations, entrepreneurs, artists, members of spiritual organizations, kids labeled "troubled," people recently released from prison, and many others—who measurably uplifted every area of their life by learning to communicate more effectively with others and themselves.

My role with my students and with you is to offer a map and to be your trusty guide or fairy godmother, guiding you to transcend any old reactive patterns so your genuine aspirations are realized.

No matter what you've experienced in life, your being is beyond any circumstance, the past, any story, or beliefs. Throughout this book, I share my own history and stories because they offer wisdom and can make a difference, but the specifics of my circumstances don't really matter. Who I Am is beyond every story. And so it is with you.

Foreword

My dear friend Niurka wisely teaches that "how you experience life mirrors the quality of your questions." When we learn to ask spiritually aerodynamic questions, we emerge from the cocoon of the limiting understanding we have of ourselves and learn to freely fly on the wings of our true nature. Think about it: until we know who and what we are, how is it possible to proceed creating a meaningful and fulfilling life?

The simple act of picking up this book indicates that you are ready to wholeheartedly participate in the richly textured events of life by placing before yourself fresh questions and receiving new insightful answers about your existence. I'm referring here to pivotal questions that just won't go away about the meaning of life beyond what we've been conditioned to believe through upbringing, culture, education, society, and religion. The time comes when we ask, "Am I moving in the direction that sup-ports my deepest evolutionary progress?"

Niurka emphasizes how the words we use—which originate in the thoughts we think—exercise a profound influence upon the actions we choose to take. She wisely encourages us to con-sciously focus the energy of language in a direction that will serve our higher purpose. Her teachings on skillful means for working with whatever spiritual, mental, and emotional challenges that arise will gently yet firmly guide you on how to let go of false perceptions, rationalizations, justifications, and well-worn excuses, replacing them with mind-sets and heart-sets that allow you to flourish in all of your life circumstances.

One of the most progressive ways to begin or deepen your pilgrimage into the nature of your true self is with a trustworthy guide, an individual who has walked the path with commitment, discipline, and joy. Niurka is such a guide, extending to us an invitation to step firmly on the path of self-discovery, for navigating the yet undiscovered inner terrain of Self.

Within the pages of *Supreme Influence*, Niurka synthesizes her own process of self-inquiry, which led her to studying the world's spiritual traditions, cognitive sciences, theories of quantum physics, and philosophy. This book is a road map to how she wholeheartedly entered her spiritual practices and transformed her life of pain and suffering into one of joy and celebration. And now you too may apply the practical and wise methods she shares for assessing the influences and habitual patterns running your life, releasing those that no longer serve you, and accelerating the energy of those that do. How reassuring it is that once you become authentic, you can never again fit back into the claustrophobic box of the past.

Niurka takes you to the root of what it means to be authentic. She sets before you a rich banquet of wise choices for manifesting your highest potential. Her artful mix of methods is a wondrous investigation into the source and importance of how to uncover your innate strength, confidence, and joy under all of life's circumstances. By applying them, you will find the

freedom of simply being yourself and responding authentically
to each moment.

Michael Bernard Beckwith
Author of *Life Visioning: A Transformative Process
for Activating Your Unique Gifts and Highest Potential*

SECTION I

ILLUMINATE

JOURNEY OF AWAKENING

You are holding this book and likely wondering . . . what is Supreme Influence?

Supreme Influence is a way of being and communicating with purpose, poise, precision, and power. It is a practice that allows you to consciously create harmonious relationships and produce successful results in every area of life.

Why is Supreme Influence important? Because we have been influenced through upbringing, society, schools, religions, media, and culture. Studies show that by the time we are 8 years old, we have had over twenty-five thousand hours of linguistic programming. Words have been downloaded to us, imprinting our minds with ideas about *who we are* and what is or isn't possible. These subconsciously ingrained beliefs fuel our thoughts and drive our behaviors *until we wake up!*

This book is a journey of awakening to a deeper understanding of *who you are* and *why you are here*. These pages offer you wisdom and practical tools to transcend reactive tendencies so you authentically embody your magnificence. You will learn advanced communication skills to improve your business, enhance your relationships, and enrich every area of your life. You will learn how to align your thoughts, focus, beliefs, body language, words, goals, and vision with your true purpose and authentic self.

Regardless of what you've experienced up until now, you absolutely can rapidly and often instantly transform challenges, realize your vision, *and* inspire others through your example. Let me share a story with you about how I discovered this for myself.

WAKING UP

At age 15 I embarked on a quest for freedom, truth, and enlightenment—except back then I called it "running away from home." I hopped on the back of a friend's motorcycle, not sure where I was going or what I would do. I just knew something had to change. I was going through a rebellious phase, resisting my parents, opposing the strict religious school I was forced to attend, and being frustrated in a world that didn't make sense to me.

So, I scribbled a runaway note, stabbed it onto a dartboard, and disappeared into the night. At the time I felt like I didn't belong, as though my parents and others surrounding me didn't see *me*, hear *me*, or care to understand. I kept asking myself, *How did I get on this planet?* I felt trapped. Alone. I didn't understand the world I was living in and felt powerless to change it. I suppose I saw only two options back then: fight or flight. After years of disagreeing and arguing—I left.

What brought me to that point? I was raised by conservative Cuban parents in Miami. I went to Catholic school and partook of confession, communion, rosaries, and penance. I sold doughnuts at Sunday morning service. I was told what was right and wrong, good and bad, moral and immoral. If my intuition led me in a different direction than the rules, I wasn't allowed to follow it.

Then, when I was 12, a traumatic event shook my family. My parents changed religion and radically changed the rules. I felt ambushed. We stopped celebrating holidays. We went to church up to three times a week. By 13 I was in a new school that didn't allow listening to rock 'n' roll music or dancing. I remember sneaking in Bon Jovi cassettes and paying the consequences in detention hall, where I was made to write countless dictionary definitions (a "punishment" that gave me glimpses of the power of words). Shorts were banned, even during physical education class, and replaced with Smurf-blue culottes. I had never heard of "culottes," and soon learned it was a divided skirt ending just below the knee. I hated playing soccer in those culottes. Actually, I hated my life. I felt confused and controlled. It didn't make sense that my parents' new way would be right and everyone else in the world following a different path would burn in hell for all eternity. I was craving answers to some major questions: *Who am I? What is my purpose? Why am I here?* I was yearning to know myself, to understand my place in the world, in the cosmos. I was longing to know God, to feel God, to understand the truth about God.

For three years I plotted my escape. Several times I packed my schoolbag with a few possessions and hid it in my bedroom closet, only to chicken out. Eventually pain outweighed fear. I could no longer follow rules and traditions without understanding their source and reason. I felt like a volcano on the brink of eruption. The angst manifested in my body as strange ailments doctors couldn't diagnose, including an engorged lower lip and a stiff neck that caused me to hunch to one side like a prettier version of the Elephant Man. I had *nothing* to look forward to, but right then "nothing" sounded a lot better than the "something" I was experiencing. I had to get out.

After leaving home, I skipped school and spent the next few weeks bouncing from place to place. With no skills or experience, just sheer determination, I acted older to get jobs. I sold gym memberships and credit card machines, hawked knives door-to-door, and worked one gig at an eclectic clothing boutique called "Ouch," which sounded like I felt, for $4 an hour in cash. I ate budget meals: 33¢-a-box mac 'n' cheese; a cup of noodles for variety. Eventually I rented a room with no furniture and saved for a futon and a TV, which turned out to have only one channel—poltergeist static.

By the time I was 16, I had officially dropped out of high school, my best friend had died, I had been raped, and I felt awful about myself and my life. Not knowing what to do, I decided to go back home. My dad was grateful; he even gave me his older red Honda Prelude. But soon home life grew disharmonious. My parents and I didn't understand how to communicate without getting upset. One day I had an argument with my mom and left the house. When I returned the next day, my books and clothes were in a bag on the front porch waiting for the donation truck pickup, and my bedroom was painted a different color. I knew deep down we all loved one another. I yearned for a way to create understanding and bridge worlds.

Once again I left home. I was grateful for my little red Prelude, which I parked across the street from the airport to watch the planes take off, pretending I was journeying to a far-off exotic land. I didn't realize it then, but watching those planes soar into the sky sparked my search for who I would become. I began visualizing myself living free and traveling the world. I saw myself riding a camel at sunrise by the Great Pyramids in Egypt. I saw myself swimming with wild dolphins in the sea. I saw pictures in my mind of the life I wanted. Feeling a surge of energy, I declared, "I will find a way to do what I want to do!" Then something inside me snapped. It felt as if my soul cracked open, unleashing a fierce resolve to find answers, feel peace, and discover a way to create a magnificent life. Beyond the chaos, I had a silent knowing that my life had a purpose—I was destined for more. I made a decision. Something had to change . . . and *I* had to change it.

My resolve created a sense of personal power and direction. Yet I had no idea what to do next. Throughout the day I recited a mantra I had read in the Bible: *Ask and you shall receive, seek and you shall find, knock and the door shall open.* I spoke these words passionately, believing an answer would come. And in a flash one did, in the form of a thought: *Go back to school and study business.* I followed this inner guidance. Before my peers graduated from high school, I had earned my high school equivalency certificate. By 17 I had enrolled in community college. I stopped watching TV and listening to the radio and let go of "friendships" that held me back. The desire for *something better* was so intense that I severed ties with my former life and dove into new environments—ones demanding more of me than I ever believed I had.

I began making conscious choices, aiming far beyond the standards of my past and saying to myself: *Whatever you feed grows and whatever you starve dies.* Investing in books became more important than buying food or clothes. James Redfield's novel *The Celestine Prophecy* gave me hope; it spoke to my inner knowledge that all things are connected and divine serendipity surrounds us when we have awareness to see it. Dale

Carnegie's *How to Win Friends and Influence People* inspired me to become a person of influence. I wanted to influence my parents, create understanding, and bridge worlds *without selling out*. I practiced what I learned, and soon my parents and I were listening instead of reacting. I realized I could communicate to get agreement instead of resistance. Before turning 18, I moved back into my parents' home.

More important than influencing others, I began influencing myself. My life became a laboratory. Reading those books awakened me to the *Supreme power language* had to *influence* my thinking and transform circumstance. "The Bible was right," I thought. "We do create with words!" I stopped complaining. I stopped blaming my parents. I stopped talking about what was "wrong." Instead I listened, opened my heart, pictured what I wanted, and spoke about it as if it were happening now. And that affirmative language worked! In my first few semesters at school I earned straight A's, won academic awards, and even got a scholarship. I became the student body president of the largest community college in the United States. My physiology shifted too. I was standing taller, breathing deeper, and feeling greater potency. I was seeing myself from a new perspective, one of love and appreciation.

A few months before finishing community college, I answered a newspaper ad for a part-time job. The interview was in a hotel. As I pulled up to the valet driving my mom's blue Monte Carlo, the car died right there in front of the hotel. Embarrassed, I walked in to my interview and saw something I had *never* seen before. One thousand excited people had also showed up in the room where my "interview" was to take place. At the head of the room, the woman onstage was wearing a white suit and jeweled ornamentation. Captivated by her presentation, I fell hook, line, and sinker for a pyramid scheme. I saw the glamour and success I thought I wanted so badly that I invested all my energy, my savings, and my credit card limit. The government shut down the company. By age 18 I was shuffling close to $40,000 in debt and my car was full of unsold water filters and vitamins.

Often the experiences that challenge us the most are the ones that harbor the greatest gifts. This challenge introduced me to the book that became my greatest mentor: *The Law of Success* by Napoleon Hill. "In every adversity lies the seed of equal or greater opportunity," Hill wrote. I devoured this text with a pen, highlighter, and journal in hand. I searched for the opportunities buried beneath my challenges. I wanted freedom, and at that time the only way I could imagine realizing it was through money. With certainty and focused intensity, I wrote down my first goal, or as Hill puts it, my "definite chief aim." I declared: "I earn $100,000 or more per year."

By age 20 I achieved my declaration. I made my first $100,000 per year while traveling the country as the top corporate trainer for Anthony Robbins (the world-renowned transformational teacher and motivational guru). By 24 I was traveling the world, riding camels by the Great Pyramids, and swimming with wild dolphins in the Red Sea, just as I imagined that day at the airport. I had proof that my external reality would shift when my internal and external communication shifted. Rapidly my whole life improved—my attitude, my relationships, my finances, my eating habits, my wardrobe, my living situation, my confidence, and my peace of mind. I was learning, achieving goals, doing what I loved, and feeling free!

.   .   .

I used my focus and language to change my life. I realized I had been raised and influenced to think, speak, and perceive the world in certain predictable ways, and although several of these beliefs served me well, many of them did not. Now I could choose beliefs that worked and contemplate, challenge, and ultimately transform those that didn't. I noticed times when constricting beliefs surfaced, but because I was aware of them, I was no longer held captive! I could ask, "Hmm, is this really true? Where did this belief come from?" Through my own experience, I understood that I could direct my focus, choose my language, and empower myself, no matter what! I wasn't a victim of circumstance. *I had the power to transform my life! I had Supreme Influence.*

That's my story. Well, part of it. What's yours? Why are you here? If you could consciously create anything in your life, what would it be? What is most important to you? What do you really want? Is it freedom? Happiness? Fulfilling work that produces prosperity? Do you want intimacy, a powerful partnership, juicy sacred love, or all of the above? Do you want to transform a recurring problem? Stop settling for less than what you are capable of? Do you want to feel lean, healthy, and energized? Be the most tuned-in, amazing parent to your beautiful child? Build your dream home or sacred sanctuary? Travel the world? What are you inspired to create? If you had a magic wand and could wave it to manifest your heart's desire instantly, what would you call forth? What if you knew that right now you have the power to summon and embody all these experiences and more? With Supreme Influence, you can!

When your thoughts, focus, physiology, expressions, language, beliefs, goals, and vision *flow* through your Supreme Self, you have power! And I don't mean power over any person or thing. I mean real power. The kind of power that *needs nothing* because it knows it has all. This is ultimate freedom, the kind that comes with living a genuine life, the freedom to be your true self and to make choices without fear. This *power* and *freedom* are the fruits of living in your Supreme Influence. Here you see with enlightened eyes, speak with a wise tongue, and embody your authentic self. Here *you* live genuinely, freely, and mightily.

We've all seen Supreme Influence in action. It's what happens when one is in the flow. It's the state of being that produces masterpieces. It's the state of grace that manifests miracles. It's pure presence and creative intelligence embodied through your unique gifts.

What exactly do I mean by *Supreme*? Let's explore the deeper meaning of this word.

Supreme refers to the authentic *you*. It describes your union with the Supreme Source of all existence. Supreme is the life force energy flowing *in* you, *as* you, and *through* you. It is the cosmic intelligence animating all that is. Supreme causes planets to revolve around the sun, caterpillars to become butterflies, and embryos to develop into babies. Supreme is breathing *you* right now and breathing me. Supreme is beating *your* heart right now and beating mine too. Supreme is the source of your presence and power, and the key to your purpose. When you honor the Supreme, you live with genuine love.

So how does *Supreme* relate to *Influence?*

Influence is the power to focus your creative intelligence and elegantly manifest your true will. You have real influence when what you think, what you say, and what you do are in harmony. "In-fluence" implies *inward fluency.* When your communication with yourself is fluid and congruent, your external circumstances morph to reflect the unity within.

SUPREME INFLUENCE IN ACTION

Supreme Influence is a verb; it is not a noun. It is a course of action. It is not a goal or destination. It is a practice. It is a way of being and communicating with yourself and the world around you. It is a sacred journey, a path to *know your self, love life, and live on purpose.*

I have been impressed with the urgency of
doing. Knowing is not enough; we must apply.
Being willing is not enough; we must do.
—LEONARDO DA VINCI

Life is about relationships. The quality of your communication determines the quality of your relationships with others and yourself. When you live in Supreme Influence, you cultivate harmonious and cooperative relationships. And it's not only how you relate with others. It's also your relationship with nature, your relationship with your life's work, your relationship with money, your relationship with food and your body temple, and most important, your relationship with *your self*. Relating in Supreme Influence allows you to manifest outstanding results in all areas of your life, such as embodying radiant health, real love, fulfilling purpose, abundant wealth, authentic beauty, and meaningful contribution. Living in Supreme Influence, you enter each relationship holistically, owning your individuality while recognizing the unity flowing through all existence.

How you experience life is a function of the choices you make. When you focus on the Supreme, you naturally make *wise choices* in thought, word, and deed that reflect who you *really* are. You will choose healthy food not because you are "trying to eat healthy" or "trying to lose weight," but because you honor your body as a temple and appreciate the earth and the life-giving power of the sun. You feel inner peace not because you took time off from work or because you meditated today, but because your life is a walking meditation. You are grateful and know everything as sacred. You have the power to confidently connect with anyone anytime, not just because you have mastered rapport skills but because you see the Supreme unity *flowing* within all things. If you act shy or self-conscious when you approach someone you would like to meet, in that moment you are not living in your Supreme Influence. Instead you can simply inhale a conscious breath, pull your shoulders back, stand up straight, and remind yourself—I am One in the

Supreme. Then imagine yourself making a genuine connection, and walk over to that person with your heart and mind in unison.

SUPREME INFLUENCE IS
CONSCIOUS INFLUENCE

Supreme Influence is conscious influence fueled with divine love and purposefully directed.

Influence happens with or without conscious awareness. Without discernment, you allow the language in the world around you to influence your thoughts and ultimately your choices, sucking you into a particular reality that may or may not be in alignment with your Supreme Influence. You will know if this happens because you feel discord. But the great news is, you can make a new choice. You can literally sidestep into a whole new realm quickly, and often instantly, simply by shifting your focus and language.

All of us were and are influenced. At an early age we began forming beliefs about God, money, sex, gender, marriage, politics, love, and morality as well as beliefs about ourselves. These inherited beliefs are often outside our conscious awareness. In other words, we are so accustomed to certain beliefs that we don't even notice them. They drive our behavior well into adulthood and can lead to unconscious reactive tendencies until we *wake up*!

Of course, many of the beliefs we pick up along the way support our personal development. For example, as a child I remember knowing I was smart. I loved to practice numbers with Count von Count on *Sesame Street*. My mom was orderly, and I enjoyed counting and (sometimes) organizing my socks, my crayons, my stickers—"One . . . two . . . three." I was also a member of a Dr. Seuss book club. I would sit on my dad's lap and read to him, while he smiled and encouraged me. Sometimes I would define a word for him, which delighted him and inspired me to learn more. My mom spoke little English, so she would ask me to translate certain things, which reinforced the empowering belief—I am intelligent.

One day my first-grade teacher hit me with a ruler and called me stupid because I misspelled my last name. But her words didn't influence me because I had a deep-seated belief: *I am smart.* In contrast, if a child is constantly told she is stupid or not good enough, then that can become an impression that will influence her life until she *wakes up.* The great news is that mental programs, like software, can be updated! We can all wake up.

You can break yourself free from your hereditary
patterns, cultural codes, and
social beliefs; and prove once and for all that
the power within you is greater than
the power that's in the world.
—MICHAEL BERNARD BECKWITH

NOW IS OUR TIME

So, beyond all stories, here we are together, in this unprecedented moment. This is an exciting time to be alive! People all over the planet are becoming more conscious and waking up to the power they do indeed have to create their reality. And *you*, my beloved soul kin, are at the forefront. Through you, Supreme consciousness is becoming aware of itself within the human experience.

Everything is connected in a unified web. Where does the air I breathe stop and the air you breathe begin? There is only One breathing. Each one of us is a unique individual expression in the kaleidoscope of existence, blessed with the freedom to choose and the power to create. As more and more of us consciously choose to live in Supreme Influence, what arises is a global landscape where the power is vested not in any one structure or way of being—but within each person. Now is our time. We have all the resources available to us—the technology, the knowledge, the community, and the human potential. We are awakening as a species; Supreme Influence is here.

2

SPEAK INTO EXISTENCE

Speech is the mirror of the soul;
as a man speaks, so is he.

—PUBLILIUS SYRUS

"Break a leg," the DJ said to me right before I was about to step onstage. I looked at him and said, "Be careful what you speak. Words have materializing power." I wasn't kidding.

"Break a leg?" I thought. What I really wanted was a recreational *break*. I'd been working around the clock on a number of projects for two weeks straight, and the little voice in my head kept saying, *Sloooow down, take a break*. That day I kept silently repeating to myself, "I *need* a break." The word *break* was flashing in my consciousness like neon lights. And so I did just that. I scheduled some recreation time to do something I had always wanted to do—get my motorcycle license. That weekend I signed up for motorcycle safety school and gave myself a break. Literally! I fell off the bike and shattered my tibia and fibula in a triple spiral fracture.

Coincidence? Perhaps, but I don't think so. I'd been successfully riding motorcycles on and off for years, *and* I just so happened to have a "break" in an enclosed parking lot, during "safety" school, while I kept telling myself I *needed* a "break"!

Have you ever said something over and over again, and then it happened?

What if you knew that whatever you thought or said could instantly materialize? How would you speak? I bet you'd be more careful and precise with your language. Suppose there was no gap between vocalization and manifestation. You'd quickly learn to ensure everything you said matched your real intention. Would you speak words of encouragement out loud if you knew it would instantaneously boost someone's performance? Would you hurl an insult at someone who cut you off in a passing car if you knew your language had the power to affect lives? Well, it does! You speak into existence. What do I mean by this? Simply that your language has creative power, especially when you speak with certainty.

In breaking my leg, I manifested the intent of my deeper desire. I allowed myself to stop working, to rest, and to enjoy recreation time. When my DJ friend said, "Break a leg," he had good intentions. He wasn't launching a curse at me. He was wishing me luck. However, the word *break* latched on to a latent thought in my own mind, and then I began looping the thought "I *need* a break." The idea of "break" was active in my field of awareness and became a self-fulfilling prophecy.

Today I would communicate differently. Instead of saying "I *need* a break" over and over again, I would envision what I *really* want and then specifically translate the picture in my mind into words. I might say, "This weekend I'm going outdoors to rejuvenate and enjoy one of my favorite sports." Do you think this easy shift in language would have influenced my focus and ultimately changed my results? You may think, "Yeah, right, Niurka; nobody talks like that." Well, if you knew that by making these simple language shifts, you could have more fun and your whole life would improve, then would you be willing to pause for a moment, get a little creative, and envision what you *truly, specifically* want before you speak it into existence? What would happen in our world if everyone communicated consciously, creatively, and clearly?

You create as you think and speak.

Be aware. What have you been speaking into existence? What pictures have you been creating in your mind? Have you been seeing and talking about what you *don't want*? Or have you been focused on what you *do want* and what you are *inspired to create*? The quality of your communication shapes the quality of your life. If one man feels stressed and continually talks about how he "*needs* to make money," chances are he will find himself in a "needy" state and without wealth. Conversely, if one woman sees herself succeeding and congruently declares herself to be a superstar and a prosperity magnet, then prosperity will likely show up. Every cell in your being aligns with what you declare. As Deepak Chopra, MD, has said, "Your cells are eavesdropping on your internal dialogue," and "Language creates your material reality."

Here's how you can apply this wisdom right now. It's simple. Before you open your mouth, create a picture in your mind of what you really want. Make the image big, bright, crisp, and colorful. Then say what you see. This creates inward fluency—your words are matching your authentic intent. You're not mindlessly talking: you are aware. You are being purposeful and precise with your language. You can pause and ask yourself, *What is ultimately most important to me in this moment? What do I really want to express or experience?* The genius artist Vincent van Gogh said, "I dream my paintings and then I paint my dreams." See results in advance, in your mind's eye. Then, with gratitude, speak about what you are inspired to do, achieve, and/or create rather than speaking about what you "need" or "have to have" or "don't want" or what "isn't happening." This simple practice will enhance every relationship in your life. For example, in business there is a colossal difference between someone who says, "I *must* make this sale" and someone who visualizes building authentic relationships and then declares: "I'm *inspired* to open this relationship."

YOU SPEAK IN MANY WAYS

When I say, "You speak into existence," I am referring to more than the vocalization of thought. For instance, we all know that our body language speaks volumes. How about the impact of our words when we write someone a note or send a text? What if someone walks into a room wearing a particular symbol, like a cross (†) or an Om (ॐ)? That's speaking too! You "speak into existence" in many ways, including:

- Thoughts
- Internal dialogue (the little voice in your head)
- Nonverbal communication (body language and speaking through actions)
- Creative visualization (the pictures, sounds, and feelings in your mind)
- Creative artistic expression (external)
- Written words (letters, e-mails, texts, blogs, tweets, contracts)
- Use of symbols (☽, ✡, $, @, or Nike's swoosh)

- Thought transference (also known as telepathy)
- Honoring the silent space (when silence speaks louder than words)

How you wield these ways of thinking and speaking shapes your life and sculpts our collective world. Supreme Influence is the act of consciously directing these ways of communicating to cocreate success.

Here's an example.

FAITH MOVES MOUNTAINS

By age 19 I was using the power of my language to evoke confidence and achieve my goals. I'd just started working for a seminar promotions company that put on events for Brian Tracy, Tony Alessandra, and other sales training gurus. My title was corporate trainer, and my job was facilitating forty-five-minute introductory workshops for sales and management teams and enrolling people in our upcoming seminars. Because of my age and inexperience, I was given the nonqualified meetings that no one else wanted. These workshops were scattered all over the outskirts of the metropolitan New York tristate area with rookie teams of three to eight people. While the other corporate trainers were living in a grand loft in Manhattan and facilitating meetings in New York City, I was camped out alone in corporate housing in Morristown, New Jersey. I would spend countless hours driving around New Jersey, New York, Long Island, Connecticut, Philadelphia, and even as far south as Delaware. I remember driving ten miles per hour behind a horse and buggy in Lancaster, Pennsylvania! Although I enjoyed the serenity of the Amish countryside, I felt like I had been sent to Timbuktu.

Despite this situation, in my mind I kept seeing myself leading workshops in the heart of New York City. On Sundays I would go into the city to immerse myself in its energy. I'd sit on a rock by the lake in Central Park and imagine myself facilitating trainings for the most powerful companies in the world. I kept visualizing what I wanted, declaring in my mind that I would succeed in the Big Apple.

Then one day a door of opportunity opened.

"Niurka!" My manager's voice bellowed on the other end of my brick-size cell phone. "How quickly can you get to Wall Street?"

"Pretty quickly," I said while pulling out my Thomas Guide map to decipher the distance. I was sitting in bumper-to-bumper traffic. "Why, what's up?" I asked.

He quickly responded, "We have a workshop scheduled on Wall Street with a major investment-banking firm in just a few hours, and David can't make it. They're expecting our top trainer, and all the other trainers are busy giving presentations. It's your chance, kiddo! Are you ready?"

"Yes," I said. I wanted to feel ready, but inside I felt scared and excited at the same time. I took a deep breath, centered myself, sat up straight, and declared—*I am ready!*

He gave me the details and our call ended. I had committed. There was no turning back. My body trembled. I felt nervous but didn't want to say it out loud. I took deep breaths, inhaling and exhaling. I pulled into a local coffee shop, sat in the parking lot for a moment, closed my eyes, and pictured myself connecting with each person in the meeting. Then I walked into the coffee shop's bathroom, brushed the lint off my velvet jacket, which I had bought at a thrift store and would recycle with my outfits. I looked in the mirror, spruced up my curly locks, and with passion declared, *"With faith the size of a mustard seed I can move mountains."*

I tell you the truth, if you have faith as small as
a mustard seed, you can say to this mountain,
"Move from here to there," and it will move.
Nothing will be impossible for you.

—MATTHEW 17:20

I was invoking "faith" (which to me meant the absence of doubt) and "moving mountains" (which to me meant achieving great success).

I drove my rental car to the transit station in New Jersey and took the underground train into the city. Then I took a subway to the financial district. When I arrived, I exited the station, marched up the stairs, and locked eyes with Wall Street's charging bull. I felt a huge rush mixed with feelings of sheer terror and profound exhilaration. I knew that this was a rite of passage. I could hear a voice inside my head say: *You are ready, Niurka! You can do this!* I kept repeating to myself, *With faith the size of a mustard seed I can move mountains.* I spoke this phrase from the depth of my being until it permeated me. I walked rapidly until I found the building. Excited and a little bit sweaty, I stepped into the elevator and declared to myself, *I have faith, and I will move mountains!*

The elevator door opened, revealing an enormous mahogany desk. The receptionist peered at me over her glasses as I introduced myself. "Hi! My name is Niurka, and I'm here to see Fred."

She looked at me coldly. "Do you have an appointment?"

"Yes," I said. "I'm the trainer scheduled to meet with him and his team."

"Reeeally? Take a seat," she said, as she picked up the phone and quipped, "Fred, Shirley Temple is here to see you."

My heart sank. I could see a flyer hanging on the wall announcing our Sales Mastery workshop that was to begin in fifteen minutes. People were trickling into the training room. As each one entered, I graciously connected with that person in my mind. Soon a tall, distinguished, silver-haired man in a dark blue pinstripe suit entered the lobby. I stood to greet him. He glanced over my shoulder as though looking for someone else. I walked over to him, held out my hand, smiled, and said, "Hi, Fred. I'm Niurka, your trainer."

He turned pale and questioned, "Are you going to do this by yourself?"

I thought I'd try some humor to create rapport. I held up my briefcase and said, "Well, Fred, I've got a little green man in here who helps me out if I get in trouble!" He was not amused. He had been promoting this event for weeks to his team of highly experienced stockbrokers and financial analysts—men and women who made hefty salaries and likely wouldn't appreciate being "trained" by a 19-year-old amateur!

Fred looked nervous as he led me into the training room. I assured him I would deliver my absolute best presentation and that everything happens for a reason. He told me to keep it short: twenty minutes max! I put my heart, mind, and soul into every word of the Five Steps to Success presentation that I had crafted by myself. At the end of my talk, I asked, "Who wants to go to the seminar?" Only one hand went up—mine. I asked again, "Seriously, who wants to go to the training seminar?" No hands. I could feel the tension in the room rising. I took a deep breath, smiled, and shared a funny story about a lumberjack who won a contest because he sharpened his ax. Then I softly asked, "Now, I'm sure someone wants to sharpen their skills and go to this seminar?"

Dead silence.

I took a deep breath, put my hand on my heart, and said, "I honor your valuable time. Please allow me to share just one last, quick story." And then a miracle happened.

Fred stood up. He looked at me, he looked at his brokers, and then he pointed at me and said, "Do you all see this kid? This kid's got balls to come in here and talk to you like this! If this seminar can get this kid to do this, then I'm going! And I think every single one of you needs to go. And if you take action right now, I'll pay for half!" About one-third of Fred's team enrolled for the seminar that day.

Fred walked me back to his office, and this time we walked side by side. He said, "You know, my daughter is about your age, and she usually comes to me for money. So I respect what you're doing."

I smiled and pounced on the opportunity. "Would you please endorse me on letterhead?"

"I'll do better than that," he chuckled. "Watch this." He thumbed through his big spiral Rolodex, picked up the phone, called a few of the other top branch managers, and gave me a glowing recommendation. The next day he escorted me onto the floor of the New York Stock Exchange. I used my focus and language to speak my vision into existence.

With faith the size of a mustard seed I can move mountains.
That day I did.

THE MORAL OF THE STORY

It's been almost two decades since Shirley Temple succeeded on Wall Street, and what I know with certainty is that you too can move mountains. You have the power to evoke and embody magnificence. You accomplish this by directing your thoughts (including the pictures in your mind), words, and actions toward your vision. This is living in Supreme Influence.

Miracles exist all around you. Miracles are expressions of love.
They happen when you are alert, ready, and available.

|||||||||||||||||||||||||||||||| **SUPREME BONUS** ||||||||||||||||||||||||||||||

Eight-Step Formula to
Craft and Deliver Dynamic Presentations

No matter how compelling your subject, the audience only embraces the message to the degree you present it authentically, clearly, dynamically, and credibly. How many times have you heard a speaker who put you to sleep? Or maybe you left a presentation entertained, but it didn't translate into significant, measurable results in your business or life. This is why it's important to have a strategy to craft and deliver your presentation with purpose, poise, precision, and power so that people are inspired to listen and take action toward a well-defined vision.

By understanding a few simple steps, you can focus your energy to deliver dynamic and influential presentations, leaving your audience entertained, inspired, and genuinely motivated to support your cause. These same steps can be applied to inspire your family, friends, clients, and colleagues to create win-win scenarios.

Are you ready? Before I give you the steps, there's a prerequisite. You want to know the answers to these questions: *How strongly do you believe in what you're saying? Why is your message vital? How committed are you to your cause? Are you on purpose? Are you inspired? Have you done your research? Have you practiced?* Your audience will champion your vision to the extent you believe in it and know what you are talking about. When you are genuinely passionate about your topic, others will be too. Remember, you can't give somebody something that you don't already have. Congruence is part confidence and part knowledge. When you know your subject inside out and you follow this eight-step framework to organize your teaching, you will speak with authority, every time. Whether you are speaking in front of a room or across the dinner table, these eight steps will ensure you speak with confidence:

Introduction and Rapport

Soften your energy for the first few moments. This ensures you align with each audience member's learning style. Thank your host. Give one or two sentences that connect with what audience members are experiencing either in the moment and/or in their business or personal lives. You can also weave in a comment about a current event that is important to this particular group. This allows you to build rapport instantly.

Little What?

Briefly state your topic: "Today I am inspired to share with you
_____." Let the audience know right away what they will be
learning from you. Summon and embody the state that you want
your audience members to experience. For example, if you want to
empower your audience, then you must emanate an *empowering*
vibe.

Why?

Explain why this topic is important to them. Be specific. Share stories, give examples, quote experts, and offer statistics that illuminate
why your message is relevant and vital. Do not move to the next step
until the audience is infused with a strong *why*—this ensures they
want to listen and you are on the same page.

Big What?

Now that your audience is connected with you, knows the topic,
and is inspired with a compelling *why*, teach them precisely what
you mean. This should be direct and simple. It helps to use visual
props.

How?

Explain how to apply this wisdom in business, life, or any other
applicable context. What specific steps should people take? This is
a great time to do a demonstration or guide the audience through
a hands-on exercise.

Suppose That...

Pose scenarios in which your lesson will be useful. You can take
audience questions here; just be clear that you will only take ques-

tions that pertain to this topic. Otherwise you'll go off point and lose your power.

Offer and Call to Action

Make sure your offer is clear and compelling and that there is a specific call to action that inspires audience members to go to the next level, like purchase a product or service, enroll in a program, offer their contact information, or any step you envision. Never have more than two main offers, because it will confuse people and they'll get paralysis by analysis. Also, it is wise to subtly plant seeds throughout your presentation that inspire the audience to want to know more.

Closing

Thank the host (if there is one) and the audience for sharing their attention and time.

This framework will ensure that you address various learning styles. For example, some people learn more visually (by seeing), others learn more auditorily (by hearing), and others learn more kinesthetically (by doing and feeling). By following the Eight-Step Formula to Craft and Deliver Dynamic Presentations, all the learning styles are recognized and honored.

Once you craft your presentation, rehearse it in your mind. See yourself successfully delivering the presentation to your audience; make the colors big, bright, crisp, and clear. Especially rehearse your talk right before going to sleep, because then your mind will integrate it while your body rests.

3

DECLARE WITH AUTHORITY

Speaking into existence isn't just about the words you choose; it's the authority with which you speak and the consciousness with which you declare.

Those who realize greatness authentically and courageously speak with purpose, poise, precision, and power. They are intentional with their words and they do not pussyfoot around. When our nation's forefathers signed their names on the Declaration of Independence, they spoke freedom and independence into existence. Their language was crystal clear, succinct, undeviating, and backed by "the Laws of Nature." On July 4, 1776, these brave men declared, "We hold these truths to be self-evident, that all men are created equal." Although at the time of this writing certain definitions of words like *men* and *liberty* were questionable, these pioneers transcended fear, spoke with might, and commanded change.

In the book of Genesis, God (whose name in this verse is Elohim [אלהים], which most closely translates into "Powers")*

---

* The word "God" describes the source of all existence, the Supreme Intelligence and Power creating and sustaining the universe, which is called by many names in different traditions.

creates the world by speaking it into existence. The English translation of Genesis 1:3 has traditionally been "Then God said, 'Let there be light,' and there was light." However, the original Hebrew transliteration of Genesis 1:3 reveals that what Elohim spoke was "Be Light." It was vocalized as a direct command, with the supremacy of the Absolute. In other words, God did not beat around the bush and say, "Hi, excuse me. Would it be okay to get a little bit of light around here?" God declared the Word succinctly, with full knowledge that it is done as it is spoken.

When you speak with authority, like our nation's statesmen who staked their lives, their fortunes, and their honor for what they believed in, you will not be denied. Fear is the only thing that gets in the way of speaking your ultimate dream life into existence. This chapter is about transcending fear and owning your creative power so that when you speak, you summon results.

WHO SPEAKS

The unexamined life is not worth living.

—SOCRATES

The beliefs you have about yourself will influence how you think and speak and determine the results you produce. Here's an example of how language and beliefs influence performance in the context of business.

The Lion and the Squirrel

For years I provided consulting and training for Mercedes-Benz. One day I was at a particular dealership in Los Angeles, California, coaching the sales team. During this session I had a conversation with the top and bottom producers—and their choice in language revealed the cause of their dissimilar results.

When I sat with the bottom producer to discern the cause of his poor performance, he spewed a litany of excuses. First he blamed the economy, asking, "Don't you read the newspaper?" Then he blamed the lack of advertising. Next he blamed the weather, saying "June gloom" was at fault, that "people don't shop for cars if the weather is bad." I had never heard of June gloom and soon learned it is a California term used to describe heavy fog that settles along the coast, obscuring the sun in early summer. Then he contradicted himself, saying, "When it's nice out, people want to be at the beach."

I listened and continued asking questions. He then claimed the managers were spoon-feeding deals to the other salesmen. "It's a dog-eat-dog world," he whined. "Haven't you been on the sales floor? It's like a shark tank down there." This guy was the king of clichés. I continued my inquiry for twenty minutes. I wasn't letting him off the hook. I listened as he aired all his excuses until finally, exasperated, he squeaked, *"All right, already! Geez! I'm just a squirrel trying to get a nut, okay?!"*

Wow! Of all the infinite number of statements that could have come out of his mouth, this metaphor illuminated his self-perception and explained his lack of confidence in business. As I looked at him more closely, he even started looking like a squirrel—puffy cheeks and all! No wonder he was producing poor results. He was unconsciously associating himself with prey scrounging for scraps!

Right then the top producer cruised into the showroom and began making his rounds. He wore a perfectly pressed black-and-gold pinstripe suit with a gold silk handkerchief, matching gold-buckled shoes, and a gold pen in his breast pocket. I looked over at the "squirrel" and asked, "How does Shapoor create his record-breaking numbers?"

"Oh, Shawn?" he said. "Well, he's been the top producer for years."

"What specifically does he do to sell so many cars?" I asked. "Tell me what is the very first thing he does when he arrives in the morning?"

"Look at him," he answered. "It's what he's doing right now. He strides in in his shiny suit and starts schmoozing. He makes people feel good. . . . Everyone loves Shawn."

I was committed to going deeper and so kept asking questions to uncover his understanding of Shapoor's beliefs and strategies. Through my penetrating questions, he was able to map out a play-by-play game plan of precisely how and what Shapoor did to achieve consistent outstanding results.

Consciously, this man knew what actions to take to increase his performance. He described a successful sales process in detail: how to create rapport, prospect, schedule appointments, follow up, get referrals, and even inspire clients to a yes. But there was a gap between what he knew intellectually and what he believed he was capable of.

Later, I coached Shapoor, asking him questions to elicit his beliefs and strategies. Interestingly, he also described himself with an animal metaphor. His head high, chest puffed out, and arms spread wide across his desk, he roared: *"This is my domain."* He was intense, and he looked me right in the eyes. "I am the Lion," he said with a growly grin. He wasn't boasting; he saw himself this way. His identity was king of the jungle and top of the food chain. And I could feel it from his royal presence. His results mirrored his statement. In just one month, I coached the Lion to increase his sales by over 50 percent while working fewer hours, and that year he became one of the top five sales professionals for Mercedes-Benz nationwide.

Both men worked in the same dealership, in the same environment, with the same potential opportunities, but their language and self-perceptions led to very different realities and vastly different results.

In the context of sales, surely it's more empowering to declare yourself a lion than a squirrel. But if the lion becomes too attached to this identity, thinking that's who he is, and predominately speaks from that space, he limits choice. Even an identity that empowers can keep you stuck in a paradigm. It is liberating to let go of who you think you are. It is possible to embrace a potent identity without hypnotizing yourself into believing that's you. Living in Supreme Influence, you can step into any empowering identity without becoming attached. Different identities will bring out different aspects of you. Freedom cannot be experienced when you are bound in any one narrow identity. Your consciousness is boundless and cannot be contained. Call yourself the lion and allow yourself to roar, but know this is merely one of many roles you can access on your human adventure.

Everyone has genius.

Turns out the "squirrel" knew himself as master of his domain on the basketball court. When he talked about the game, his demeanor shape-shifted. His puffy cheeks relaxed, his eyes narrowed in focus, and an aura of confidence emerged. Through our coaching sessions, he owned his tremendous strengths and gifts and learned how to transfer his skills and determination from the basketball court into his business to create success.

THE MORAL OF THE STORY

There are several lessons to be harvested from this story. One main lesson is: Whatever you declare after the words *I am*, that is what you create, attract, and become, especially when you speak with conviction. "I am" is a statement of identity.

Notice how you describe yourself. What do you say after the words *I am?* Your response shapes how you see yourself, how others see you, and what's possible for you.

Get curious. Are your "I am" statements emerging from fear or certainty? When you describe yourself, are you boasting or trying to look good for others, or are you sharing your genuine sentiments. Do you more frequently say things that disempower or empower you? Do you say things like "I'm stressed, I'm bored, I'm tired, I'm disappointed, I'm broke, I'm stupid, I'm alone, I'm depressed, I'm out of shape, I'm angry"? Or do you say, "I am centered, I am inspired, I am brilliant, I am focused, I am on a roll, I am pure genius, I am ready, I am grounded, I am sexy, I am loving my life, I am grateful, I am a creator! I am one with God, and God is everything."

A profound insight into the words *I am* is revealed in the Torah. In Exodus 3:14, Moses asks God for his name. And God responded, "ehyeh ašer ehyeh" (אהיה אשר אהיה). The closest translation is: I AM that I AM. Consider that when you use the words *I am*, you may be invoking the power of the Supreme. These words—*I am*—are potent. Be aware of what you link them to. The thing you're claiming has a way of reaching back and claiming you.

Applying this wisdom to your life is simple. Be sure that when you say the words *I am* that you authentically mean what you say afterward. Choose words that call forth the best in you.

Here's a powerful practice. When you wake up in the morning, declare what you are grateful for. Begin with the words *I am*. For example: *I am grateful for my beautiful family. I am grateful for* _____. Do this daily ritual for five minutes every morning, and be specific.

4

WHO AM I?

Knowing others is intelligence;
knowing yourself is true wisdom.

—LAO TZU

In my early teens, I studied the Dhammapada, a masterpiece of early Buddhist literature and the most succinct expression of the Buddha's teaching. Within its pages was a quote that sparked my quest for divine understanding. It said, "The only effort of any intelligent person in this world should be, first and foremost, how to know something which cannot be destroyed by death." These words awakened my profound desire *to know that which transcends death, to understand that which is real.*

I knew that one day my body would die, that we all face death, that everything in the material world was transient. I figured no other question was relevant or worth asking if I couldn't answer this fundamental question: *What is it that transcends death?*

I needed to know for myself. I was done having people tell me what I should or shouldn't believe about God or my own soul. I felt anxious and confused about religion and the afterlife. Answering existential questions became the crux of my late teens and twenties. Nothing was more important. My second priority was creating the financial success that would afford me the independence to explore and discover these answers in style. I decided I would never know how to live powerfully if I didn't know how to die, and I would never know how to die if I couldn't answer this riddle. I had to know—*Who am I? What is my purpose? Why am I here?* For me, there was no other option.

I'm sure you too have asked profound questions. One of the most important questions you could ask is . . . *Who am I?* Notice what feelings and images this question evokes in you. Observe the first answer that comes to mind. Get curious. Take out your journal. Ask yourself, *Who am I?* Write down your thoughts. Now look at what you wrote. Notice how your responses make you feel. How you answer this question determines the degree of power fueling your thoughts, words, and actions.

This question can be answered on many levels. Would you state your name? Would you identify with a role or part you play (e.g., I am a mother, a friend, a coach, an artist, a doctor, or an entrepreneur)? Does your primary answer emerge from the realm of personality or from someplace deeper? Would you tune in to the infinite Source that animates your life and speak from this silent knowing? Would your answer reflect that who you are cannot be contained by any one role, even though you play many? Or would you identify more with qualities about yourself (e.g., I'm smart; I'm tall, dark, and handsome; I'm a single dad)? Would you refer to your profession (I'm a Realtor or a lawyer)? Or would you identify with your accomplishments (I'm a third-degree black belt in aikido)? Or would you relate more with the past (I'm a cancer survivor)?

Who are YOU?

—CATERPILLAR IN *ALICE'S ADVENTURES IN WONDERLAND*

What you create in the midst of infinite possibilities will match your "I am" statements. This means that the results you produce will not exceed what you say about yourself.

For example, one of my students yearned for a deeper connection with his children but didn't know how to create it. He had immigrated to the United States and spent most of his time working to provide his family with the quality of life he never had as a child. I asked him, "Who are you in relationship with your children?" He nodded his head and said, "I'm the disciplinarian." I asked him to elaborate. He said his wife was the nurturer, and his job was to mold his boys into men. He explained how he was harsh and demanding, just like his father had been with him, and he had dreaded behaving like his father. He loved his children but didn't know how to express it. As he told me this story in tears, I worked with him to expand his self-perception, to free himself from the confines of this limited way of seeing himself and communicating with his boys. Through questions I guided him to uncover what he really wanted, at the deepest level. He came to realize that he had choice on how to relate to, respond to, and guide his children. And that love matters most. Together we discovered new affirmative ways to meet his true intention.

We cannot teach people anything; we can only
help them discover it within themselves.

—GALILEO

You speak into existence from your sense of self. If you are anchored in any one specific identity, then you will think, speak, and create from that particular role.

You are a multidimensional being. Like a diamond, you are multifaceted. For example, a woman can be a mom, daughter, entrepreneur, philanthropist, investor, athlete, artist, teacher, and queen. She can be all of these and more. A man is multidimensional too. He can be a dad, son, leader, athlete, lover, poet, and king. Supreme Influence declares that who you are is Supreme. Your consciousness cannot be encapsulated by any one identity. You can enjoy and explore myriad identities even as you realize that *your* authentic being is not defined by any one of them.

When I found out who I really was, I discovered
that I am not in the Mind, but the Mind is in me. I'm
not in the body, but the body is in me. I'm not in the
world, but the world is in me. Curving back within
myself, I create again and again. In essence, I Am
That which creates all of That—I Am That, you are
That, All this is That, and That's All there Is. If you
find That, then you have it All.

—THE VEDAS

As a drop of water is to the ocean, you are one in the sea of Supreme consciousness. You are an irreplaceable gift. There has never been and there will never be anyone or anything like you. You are a phenomenon, a miracle, a marvel. Nothing in the entire cosmos has ever had or will ever have your particular perspective and your unique way of shining your light into the world. Simply put, you are a Supreme emanation of the Universe, whole and complete in every way, perfect in your own imperfection.

REMEMBER THE SOURCE OF
YOUR PRESENCE AND POWER

Learning is remembering.

–SOCRATES

By 20, I was practicing Jñāna yoga, the path of knowledge. I studied ancient wisdom texts including the Bible, Bhagavad Gita, Tao Te Ching, Kabbalah, and others; I studied new thought teachings, including Science of Mind and the Course in Miracles. I searched for essential truths buried within parables, sutras, riddles, and stories. I would compare my own experience with my research, cross-referencing sources, deciphering correspondences, and relating the truths of ancient texts to recent discoveries in quantum physics and cognitive neuroscience. I've sat in contemplation and meditation, and communed with great masters. My quest for knowledge grew into a sacred love affair with life. I have come to know that we are here to be, feel, create, evolve, and love, and that when we genuinely love, we are Supreme.

My journey awakened me to realize that the anthropomorphized God I had been looking for throughout my early years was quietly hidden *within* all along, patiently awaiting my discovery and attention. Owning this realization—*I Am*—is the key to transcending fear so you speak with authority and consciously create what you envision.

So how do you speak with authentic power, not just once in a while but consistently? First, believe. *You are Supreme.*

Regardless of your spiritual beliefs or which religious organization you belong to (or not), there is affirmation everywhere
when you're open to it. Here is some of what the great spiritual traditions say about you: The Gospel according to Luke
17:20–21, referring to Genesis 1:26–27, says, *"Behold, the kingdom of God is within you."* The kingdom of heaven is not outside
you. It is not a destination to be attained. It is not a reward
given to those "worthy" after death. It is an internal realization.
The kingdom of heaven and all the wonders you could ever
desire reside within you! The majesty of our universe is alive
in you now! This means that love, joy, wisdom, prosperity, and
peace are your birthright. You are a Supreme being, made in the
"image and likeness of God."

   The great sages of ancient India revealed: *aham brahmasmi,*
which means "all that exists is within me." The English translation of this Sanskrit sutra is "the core of my being is the ultimate reality, the root and ground of the universe, the source of
all that exists."

   "Know yourself, and you will know the Universe" is an
alchemical axiom. In Hermetic alchemy (the science and art of
conscious transformation) there is a foremost tenet: "As above,
so below. As within, so without. As in the microcosm, so in the
macrocosm."

   What do these passages reveal? You and the Supreme are
one. This realization is what energizes your thoughts and words
with authority and creative power! Living in this awareness is
the true purpose of yoga. It is the reason for meditation. It is
the meaning of enlightenment and self-realization. Communicating from this unshakable space is Supreme Influence in
action.

You are gods, children of the Most High,
all of you.

—PSALMS 82:6

"Know thyself," as Lao Tzu declared, is not merely an intellectual understanding of identity. It's not something static you find or define. "Know thyself" is *an experiential knowing* paradoxically existing in the mystery. The key to know yourself as Supreme is to let go of the idea that you need to find something that isn't already present. Relax into the wisdom of your own being. That which you seek is you.

That which permeates all, which nothing
transcends and which, like the universal space
around us, fills everything completely from within
and without, that Supreme non-dual Brahman—
That thou art.

—SANKARACHARYA

There is an ancient Buddhist story that speaks of the time when the Buddha wandered in northeastern India shortly after his enlightenment. He encountered several men who recognized him to be an extraordinary being. They asked him: "Are you a god?" "No," he replied. "Are you a reincarnation of god?" "No," he replied. "Are you a sage, then?" "No." "Well, are you a man?" "No." "So what are you?" the perplexed men asked. Buddha simply replied, "I am awake." *Buddha* means "the Awakened One."

In Buddhism, the Lotus Sutra, one of the great teachings, says that Buddhahood (a state of Supreme enlightenment) is inherent within each of our lives. The eleventh-century Buddhist monk Nichiren Daishonin wrote, "When deluded, one is called an ordinary being, but when enlightened, one is called a Buddha." Nichiren further wrote, "If you seek enlightenment outside yourself, then you're performing even ten thousand practices, and ten thousand good deeds will be in vain."

Supreme Influence is available to us all. The Universe does not play favorites. It responds equally to thought vibration. What you sow is what you reap. When you plant tomato seeds, you don't get eggplant. When you mix the colors yellow and blue, what color do you get? You get the color green. We all get green. The Universe doesn't give some of us green and not others.

THE LOGOS (WORD)

This book reveals a formula for conscious creation through language. In previous chapters, we spoke about creating vivid pictures in your mind, then matching your words to your pictures and speaking them into existence. This chapter reveals how you can speak with authentic authority by owning your "I am" presence and power. Now let's consider a model of possibility that shows this wisdom in action.

Logos is a Greek word (λόγος) meaning "the Living Word" or *creative sound vibration* from which our entire experience of reality has been shaped and continues to evolve. Stoic philosophers identified the Logos as the "divine animating life principle of the cosmos." Logos represents Supreme Will speaking into existence. It is the fundamental intelligence through which we create as we speak, through organized thought and vocalization. *Ordo ab chao* is Latin for "order out of chaos." Order is called forth from chaos through Logos. Without Logos nothing manifests. Therefore, how do we come to understand, integrate, and wield the power of this mighty omnipresent cosmic principle—Logos, the Word—into our daily lives? The answer to this question is revealed to you within the pages of this book.

In the beginning was Brahman,
with whom was the Word;
and the Word was truly the
Supreme Brahman.

—RIG VEDA

In the beginning was the Word,
and the Word was with God,
and the Word was God.

—JOHN 1:1

In the Gospel according to John 1:14, Jesus (whose Hebrew name, Yeshua, means "the Living One Saves") is described as the incarnation of the Logos. "The Word became flesh and made his dwelling among us." Through Jesus's example, we are guided to activate the Logos in our own lives and to anchor Supreme Influence in the human experience.

According to the Bible, Jesus spoke miracles into existence because he was one with God. In Matthew 9:1–8, Jesus heals a paralytic man. Speaking with the authority of the Absolute, Jesus declares the man's sins forgiven and tells him to get up and walk, and the man walked. Jesus declared in John 14:12 that you too can accomplish this: "I tell you the truth, anyone who believes in me will do what I have done and even greater things." In John 14:20 he said, "On that day you will know that I AM in my Father, and you are in me, and I AM in you." What do these passages reveal? How is it that a God-man could wield the natural forces to walk on water and multiply loaves of bread and fish, then say we too have access to this Supreme power? Because we do!

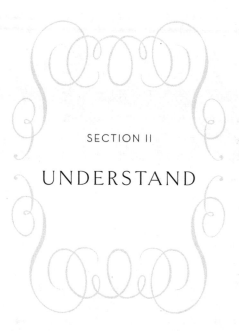

SECTION II

UNDERSTAND

5

NLP COMMUNICATION MODEL

One of the pillars of my life's work is the study of NLP (neuro-linguistic programming), an approach to communication, psychotherapy, and personal development. NLP explores the relationship between how we think (*neuro*), how we speak (*linguistic*), and our patterns of behavior and emotion (*programming*). In this chapter we explore the NLP communication model to illuminate how we each create our own experience of reality. This understanding will help you make wiser choices regarding what you focus on and the meaning you give to the experiences in your life.

Let's look at the deeper meaning behind neuro-linguistic programming:

> **Neuro:** Refers to neurology and the ways in which our brains and nervous systems process information through our five senses: sight (visual), hearing (auditory), touch (kinesthetic), smell (olfactory), and taste (gustatory).
>
> **Linguistic:** Language and other nonverbal communication systems through which our experiences, memories, and visions are coded, ordered, and given

meaning. This includes pictures, sounds, feelings, smells, tastes, and internal dialogue.

Programming: The way we code, store, and represent our experiences within our neurological systems.

NLP is an evolving body of work, and its ultimate purpose is to study, describe, and transfer models of human excellence.

MY EARLY DAYS WITH NLP

At 19 I would sit in the audience watching my then boss Tony Robbins miraculously transform people's lives, and I knew unequivocally what my purpose was. I witnessed lifelong phobias dissolve. I saw couples on the verge of separation let go of grievances and authentically connect. I observed families heal and transcend circumstances that they couldn't see beyond before. I watched a person contemplating suicide change his mind on the spot and become grateful for the gift of life. Like a linguistic Jedi, Robbins could reframe any problem into a possibility. This intrigued me at a deep level. I was enthralled by *conscious transformation*.

Captivated and fascinated, I knew I wanted to understand the mind-body-spirit connection. I wanted to help people move beyond the greatest challenges in their lives and create victory. I wanted to connect the dots between science and spirituality. And so this part of my life's journey began as I mastered the study of NLP. It was during this time that I realized NLP's profound connection with quantum physics, computer science, psychology, and ancient wisdom, all of which inspired the creation of Supreme Influence.

Here's a little history.

NLP emerged in 1975 when Richard Bandler (a mathematician) and John Grinder (a transformational linguist) at the University of California at Santa Cruz began studying the world's most successful communication experts. By examining how these geniuses produced consistent, outstanding results, Bandler and Grinder reverse-engineered the communication strategies of Fritz Perls, Virginia Satir, and Milton Erickson, three of the most prominent and accomplished psychotherapists alive at the time. As the two men studied these linguistic wizards and translated their approaches into duplicable models, the NLP communication model was born.

INTERNAL REPRESENTATIONS AND THE NLP COMMUNICATION MODEL

Billions of bits of information surround you. You live in a universe of infinite possibility! You experience this world through your senses; however, your brain and nervous system don't consciously process it all. It's too much data. So what you (and I and everyone else) do all day long is sort through this endless sea of waves and particles and pay attention to only a small percentage of what's going on. We group similar things together and then re-present bite-size bits of data back to ourselves as internal representations. Internal representation (IR) is what we see, hear, and feel in our own mind; the pictures, sounds, and feelings that emerge within our own consciousness. Internal representations influence communication and drive behavior.

These IRs are linked in a web of neuro-associations, which are coded and stored as beliefs, values, and memories that

commingle with our physiology, language, and focus to generate our behavior.

We'll explore the concept of IRs more in depth in the next
chapter. Right now, let's illustrate how IRs fit within the NLP
communication model.

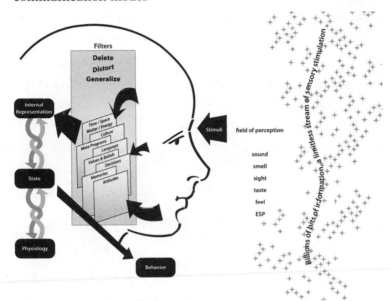

As you look at the illustration above, imagine yourself at the
center of a sensory universe surrounded by billions of stars, all
permeating your senses twenty-four hours a day with things you
can see, hear, smell, taste, feel, and sense.* The lens of your
perceptive awareness is large enough to receive the vast amount
of information, but as the original data are transmitted to your
mental filing system, deletions and distortions occur as incom-
ing stimuli search for appropriate "meaning" categories based
on your map of reality. This organization of information leads

---

* The illustration above is my own rendition of the traditional NLP communication model.

to generalizations that influence your perspective of the universe and how you behave in it.

According to Richard Bandler, the three primary filters determining how we process the limitless sensory data in our field of awareness are neurological (our physical senses), social (our family and cultural indoctrination), and individual (our beliefs and personal history). We filter the world through these constraints while deleting and distorting large chunks of information. We then create our own unique *map of reality*.

In *The Structure of Magic*, Bandler wrote:

> *We as human beings do not operate directly on the world.*
> *Each of us creates a representation of the world in which*
> *we live—that is, we create a map or model, which we use*
> *to generate our behavior. Our representation of the world*
> *determines to a large degree what our experience of the*
> *world will be, how we will perceive the world, what choices*
> *we will see available to us.*

A *map of reality* is not *reality* any more than a map of the Milky Way galaxy is the Milky Way galaxy. A mental map, similar to a geographic map, contains deletions, distortions, and generalizations—all sorts of details are missing. The quality of these maps determines how well we make sense of and navigate through our lives.

The truth of a theory is in your mind,
not in your eyes.
—ALBERT EINSTEIN

You are the mapmaker. Your map of reality represents the ever-evolving sum total of your internal representations—your beliefs, memories, imaginings, and visions. Your map is constantly being revised with new information as you grow and journey through life. Your map is not static. And you are the only person with your particular map.

STEPPING OUTSIDE OF YOUR MAP OF REALITY

If you've ever felt stuck in a "challenge," then you may have been mistaking your map for reality. As soon as you expand your awareness, new options become available. You can do this as easily as allowing your vision to open into the periphery. Step back and observe. You are the witness. From this space of expanded awareness you can choose to focus on possibilities, *while simultaneously remaining in peripheral vision.*

Let's do a quick exercise to help you step outside of your map and gain greater perspective and resources.

Pretend you are in a movie theater, sitting all the way in back. On the screen is a person who looks like you experiencing a problem. However, you are not disturbed; you are sitting back and enjoying popcorn while objectively watching the person on the screen. Notice how you gain new distinctions as you observe the situation. You also have a remote control. At any time you can make the movie go faster or slower, you can rewind or speed up. You can make it black and white, zoom in on certain areas, or blur it out. You can even watch the movie from the projection booth. Continue rolling the movie until the person on the screen gets past the problem and arrives at a moment of learning and successful resolution. Then pause the movie and unify yourself with the "you" on the screen. Now, what's different?

Solutions, possibilities, and opportunities are always present. But sometimes we don't recognize them because the mind deletes, distorts, and generalizes reality.

DELETE, DISTORT, AND GENERALIZE REALITY

Imagine a tree. A tree offers a huge amount of perceptible information. We could observe its genus, the shape of the leaf and bark, its age and height. We could examine its ecosystem, which animals live in symbiosis, and where on Earth it grows. We could inhale the tree's fragrance and recognize that the tree has certain uses, such as lumber, essential oil, or medicinal properties. We could observe the health of the tree or discover it would be great for climbing or building a tree house. Your brain would not process all the information about the tree in one take; rather, you would pick up the bits corresponding to your map.

How you delete, distort, and generalize (DDG) reveals your perspective—your references and education about trees, your imagination, your state, and more. How you perceive and then store your experience of the tree in your memory reflects less about the tree and more about your own perception.

A fool sees not the same tree
that a wise man sees.

—WILLIAM BLAKE

Let's investigate the process known as deletion.

Deletions

A deletion occurs when your brain skips over information.

Several years ago John Assaraf, an entrepreneur, researcher, and explorer of consciousness, spoke at one of my seminars. He guided an audience of five hundred people through a simple and fun exercise that showed how our minds delete information that surrounds us. John played a seventy-five-second video featuring two teams passing two basketballs. One team wears white shirts and passes the ball only to other people on their team. The other team wears black shirts and does the same. He asked the audience to focus on the team in the white shirts and count how many times they passed the ball. In the middle of the video, someone in a full-body gorilla suit walks out into the middle of the players, pounds her chest, then strolls off camera. Most of the audience deleted the gorilla. When John asked, "Did you see the gorilla?" he got blank stares. People were so focused on counting that they missed the seemingly obvious gorilla.*

This illustrates a profound point: You are surrounded by "gorilla opportunities." Sometimes you may not see them because you are focused on something else, and therefore your brain "deletes" them. Imagine expanding your consciousness and becoming even more aware of the gorilla opportunities surrounding you in your life right now.

Here's one simple way to accomplish this. Ask yourself expansive questions like: "How can I be even more aware of the opportunities surrounding me right now? Who can I collaborate

* In 1997 Christopher Chabris and Daniel Simons met at Harvard University and collaborated on research. In 2004 they received the Ig Nobel Prize in Psychology, awarded for "achievements that first make people laugh, and then make them think," for the experiment that inspired *The Invisible Gorilla* video.

with right now to achieve our goals?" If a challenge arises, you could ask, "What can I learn from this?"

In chapter 14, we will discuss the power of questions, and at that point I'll give you a formula to craft your own empowering questions. For now, let's look into the process of distortion.

Distortions

A distortion occurs when your brain processes information but substitutes one thing for another.

In 1949 researchers at Harvard University created a study testing a person's response when quickly shown playing cards with jumbled colors and suits. For example, a black three of hearts and a red six of spades would be mixed with traditional cards like a red five of hearts and a black seven of spades. The researchers discovered the subjects were so accustomed to seeing traditional cards that when colors and suits were mixed, many participants would distort the image. When shown a black three of hearts, for example, some subjects would see it as a red three of hearts, some would see it as purplish, and others would be so confused they couldn't identify the card.

What does this tell us? NLP says that people do not respond to reality; they respond to their map of reality. When something in your awareness does not match your mental map, your brain can distort it, conforming reality to the familiar. The mind stores data based on the law of association, which means the mind groups similar things together. If something unfamiliar comes to you, and you don't have internal references to associate it with, you may distort it.

If you've ever said something like, "I could have sworn he said his name was Paul!" when the name was Peter, your brain made a distortion. Or if you reached into your closet to grab a blue shirt and suddenly you realize the shirt you thought blue was actually green, your brain made a distortion.

Here's a powerful practice to expand awareness. If something challenges you, *get curious*. Rather than assigning meaning to an experience, you can step back (literally) and view the situation from different angles. Ask yourself, "What else could this mean?" You could momentarily step into another person's shoes and see things from his or her perspective. Then put your "sensory acuity hat" on! This is something I say to my students to remind them to be in the present moment and to activate their senses, as if they were a superhero. Sensory acuity allows you to recognize subtle distinctions in the sights, sounds, feelings, smells, tastes, and sensations around you.

Now let's explore how we generalize.

Generalizations

A generalization occurs when your brain deletes and distorts information and then groups it together with details missing.

Generalizations can be used purposefully. For example, if you believe the generalization "I *always* find a way when I am committed," reality will bend to your will. Your map becomes a self-fulfilling prophecy.

The words *always* and *never* are "universal quantifiers." They are generalizations, creating the experience of a perpetual static reality, which limits the possibility of something different materializing.

Pause for a moment. Consider one generalization that you've thought or spoken that no longer serves your magnificence. For example, if someone says: *Relationships take a lot of work.* Or if a person makes a generalization about him or herself: *I'm too young* or *I'm too old.* The generalization could be about someone else: *You never listen.* These generalizations cloud vision and lead to poor choices. Be aware. Ask yourself, "Does thinking and speaking this way feel good? Does it give me authentic power? Does it uplift others?" Then consciously choose generalizations that empower you, such as "I am an infinite being of love and light" or "all the power that ever was and ever will be is here now." Write down these empowering statements. Phrase your wording penetratingly and succinctly. For example, "I am on purpose," or "I succeed." Make sure you believe that what you are writing is possible. After all, when you write (and speak), you are casting a form of spell . . . that's why it's called *spelling.*

Generalizations influence perception and behavior. A few examples of generalizations include: "Politicians are shysters." "Attorneys are liars." "Police officers always eat doughnuts and drink coffee during their shift." Or "Spiritual people don't care about making money." If a person makes the generalization that spiritual people don't care about making money, and that person identifies herself as spiritual, then she may unconsciously sabotage her efforts to attract money.

HONORING AND ENTERING ANOTHER'S MAP

We each delete, distort, and generalize reality differently based on our mental maps. Honoring each person's map of reality, even if you don't agree with or understand it, is living in Supreme Influence. Saint Augustine says it well, "Love, and do what you like." Your true purpose does not infringe on the will of another.

There are a thousand ways to kneel and kiss the ground;
there are a thousand ways to go home again.

—RUMI

The Bible in John 8:1–11 relates a story where the townspeople approach Jesus about what to do with a woman they called a sinner. The people wanted to stone her to death, but Jesus instructed, "Let him who is without sin cast the first stone." The deeper meaning of the word *sin* translates as "to miss the mark" in Hebrew. If someone "sins," they have made a mis-take, or *missed the mark*. A mistake is not something to be criticized or condemned, rather it is to be understood and the course corrected. If you are driving down the freeway and suddenly realize you've missed your exit (or *missed the mark*), you don't keep driving the wrong way and you don't pull over and freak out. You check your navigation, reroute, and then forge ahead toward your destination.

Multiple paths can lead you to the same destination. Challenges in communication happen when someone mistakes his map for reality itself, making his way "right" and other ways "wrong." When an individual projects his map onto others, it can cause conflict in families, organizations, communities, and nations. Seek to understand maps and not judge them. From a state of curiosity, you can step into another's map—seeing, hearing, and feeling from her perspective—which gives you insight into how to more effectively speak into her listening style and negotiate in a reasonable way.

When we come from a space of genuine love, we let go of the need to control others or to have their maps conform to ours. We accept the fact that other people have methods that work for them, even if these ways differ from our own. We release the attachment to being right. We appreciate and learn from our differences.

The more you are motivated by Love,
the more fearless and free your action will be.

—DALAI LAMA XIV

6

THE DEEPER MEANING
OF WORDS

One of the greatest barriers to communication is assuming that it has happened! Have you ever felt certain you communicated clearly, yet the other person received an entirely different message than what you meant to convey? This chapter shows you how to more effectively translate your thoughts into words so you achieve authentic understanding. You will also become more aware of how others receive your communication and learn how you can ask questions that elicit the deeper meaning beyond the words they use. This wisdom enables you to minimize misinterpretations, so you can genuinely connect and collaborate with anyone, anytime.

Let me share a funny example of the challenges that can arise while communicating with another person and the importance of understanding the deeper meaning of words.

TITANIC MISCOMMUNICATION

Once upon a time I was scheduled to speak on a Caribbean cruise ship. It was a transformational conference at sea with speakers and luminaries who would share their wisdom. I hadn't been on a cruise since I was a child, and I imagined it would be fantastical and opulent.

As my boyfriend and I were packing our suitcases, I had romantic visions of a grand ballroom with elegant ladies in flowing gowns descending wide splendid staircases and greeted by refined gentlemen in tuxedos. I recalled a scene in the movie *Titanic* when the character played by Kate Winslet floated down the staircase to meet her beloved, played by Leonardo DiCaprio. The thought of creating my own timeless romantic scene, with me in my gown and my boyfriend in his finest tux, was enchanting. I said to him, "Honey, this will be amazing. It will be just like the *Titanic*!"

He looked at me in horror. "The *Titanic*? Are you crazy? I don't want to go on a cruise if it's like the *Titanic*!"

I said, "Didn't you see the movie?"

"Yes!" he quipped. "Almost everybody on the *Titanic* died!"

Then we broke out in peals of laughter. To him, the word *Titanic* conjured images of floating corpses in the icy North Atlantic sea. To me, the word *Titanic* lit up images of elegance, majesty, and soul mate love. Our internal representations for the word *Titanic* were completely different.

Had we not been present, playful, and willing to communicate, this misunderstanding could have escalated. Someone else (in the absence of Supreme Influence) could have reacted with disappointment or anger, projecting negative emotions and asking insecure questions like "Why doesn't he want to go on a romantic cruise with me? What's wrong with him, or what's wrong with me?"

Have you ever experienced a disproportionate reaction over a mix-up like this? Or has someone else reacted disproportionately toward you? If so, here's a simple practice for living in Supreme Influence.

Put on your sensory acuity hat. Brilliant communicators are aware of how their communication is received. One of the presuppositions of NLP is "My communication is the response I get," which means: *take ownership* of how your communication lands in another's listening. When you speak, be present to the subtle shifts in the other person's breathing, voice cues, and body language. In the example above, when I used the word *Titanic*, I was intending to be sweet, playful, and romantic; instead my communication caused my boyfriend to panic and pull away. Regardless of the response you receive, remember that you are *response-able*, which means you are *able* to *respond* in a healthy, honorable way, no matter what. Invest a moment to inhale a deep breath (or two) before responding. Then genuinely ask a purposeful question, one designed to elicit the deeper meaning beyond words. For example, my boyfriend could have asked, "Honey, *how do you mean* it will be just like the *Titanic?*" and then listened. That question would have caused me to reveal more of my romantic fantasy.

The single biggest problem in communication
is the illusion that it has taken place.
—GEORGE BERNARD SHAW

Interestingly, our actual cruise reflected none of our initial perceptions. It was a family-themed budget cruise ship with flashy Las Vegas–style lights and all-you-can-eat fried-food buffets, hardly my picture of regal living. No gown, no splendid staircase, just one titanic miscommunication.

WORDS: THE BUILDING BLOCKS OF OUR COMMUNICATION

Words are building blocks from which we piece together our communication. But unlike blocks, words are intangible. They are fundamentally abstract. A word represents something, but it is not the thing itself. A word is a sign that points to what it represents. As Aristotle said, "Spoken words are the symbols of mental experience."

Here's a quick example. Think of a dog. As you think of a dog, do you have a picture? Is it a big dog or a small dog? Does it have long hair or short hair? Notice that the image in your mind has structure. Is it in color or black and white? Is it near or far? Is it clear or blurry, bright or dim? Is it a movie or a still frame? What other images come up as you think about a dog? What does the word *dog* mean to you? There are myriad possibilities that you could conjure in your imagination. Each person will have a completely different image of the word *dog*, based on his or her own life experience. Some people see big, hairy, scary dogs, and others envision small, cuddly pets. Others may see a photograph or perhaps an animation of a dog. What did you see, hear, and feel as you thought of a dog? Whatever you conjured is your internal representation.

The word *dog* is not a dog, but it is a handy representation that allows us to communicate. When I say "dog," you have a general idea of what I mean, even if you aren't picturing the same dog I am. The word *dog* is a label, a shortcut in communication.

Language is originally and essentially
nothing but a system of signs or symbols,
which denote real occurrences, or
their echo in the human soul.

—CARL JUNG

WORDS ARE THE TIP OF THE ICEBERG

In written and spoken language, words stand in for an entire mental construct, which is different for each person. This means that when we communicate, we use *words* in an attempt to convey multilayered images, sounds, and sensations that exist within our mind. Therefore, words are like the tip of an immense iceberg, revealing what's on the surface of deep, rich internal representations. Masters of Supreme Influence do not *assume* they know what someone means when they speak; rather, they pay attention, honor the other person's map, politely ask questions, listen, and create understanding.

For example, if someone tells you he wants to "build a magnificent house," well, that's just the tip of the iceberg. You don't know what that means at all—his words are too vague. If you want to support that person, it's important to discover what's beneath the surface. You can ask, "How will you know it's a 'magnificent house'? What will you see? What will you hear and feel that lets you know it's magnificent? What specifically do you mean when you say 'build'?" In NLP the term used to describe these types of questions is "meta-model," which refers to a set of language patterns that you can use to elicit someone's map of the world and gain a fuller representation of their experience. In a moment I'll introduce a few additional meta-model questions. First let's consider what happens when people get too attached to labels and don't earnestly look beneath the surface.

LOOK BENEATH THE SURFACE

Imagine how many people have suffered and died at the hands of groups who dogmatically declared *their* "God" as the only way, while condemning others. The word *God* is the tip of the iceberg; it's a *symbol* that points to the infinitely profound, quintessential, ineffable source of existence. Here's an interesting insight into the deeper meaning of the word *God*. When I began studying ancient wisdom traditions and looking beneath the surface, I found it illuminating to realize that the Bible was originally written in Hebrew, Aramaic, and Greek. The English language did not even exist during the time of the early Biblical writings! Technically, the word *God* was not used even once in original Biblical texts! In the book of Genesis, when "God" creates the world by speaking it into existence, the original Hebrew word used for "God" in this context was "Elohim" (אלהים). There is no English translation for "Elohim." Every translation of "Elohim" is an interpretation, including mine. The closest translation I have found is "Powers," which is plural. Since Hebrew is a verb-driven language, "Elohim" was not describing a noun (such as a patriarch sitting on a throne in the sky) as much as it was a verb, or a creative process, since Elohim was in the act of creating. Hence, the Elohim are *Creative Powers*. Since we are made in the image and likeness of Elohim, we too are creative powers. Looking beneath the surface, we realize our splendor and beauty (the *I Am*). This was a monumental aha for me; it influenced how I knew my self and how I experience and commune with the Supreme Source of all existence, i.e., *God*.

So words are more than *just* words. They have history and depth. They have hidden powers that most of us didn't know about (until now). This realization captivated me and inspired my devotion to decrypt the power at the heart of language. I wanted to come as close as possible to the original source and meaning of the most profound texts and traditions. Kabbalah, for example, which is ancient Judaic mysticism exploring the nature of existence and the relationship between the macrocosm and microcosm, connects each of the twenty-two letters of the Hebrew alphabet to an image and a number. Thus there are layers upon layers of meaning imbued in every word. Let's consider just one letter: the third letter of the Hebrew alphabet, gimel (ג), corresponds to "camel." The letter pictorially represents a camel, the presence associated with bringing someone safely across the desert, or the abyss, which represents the apparent gulf between the material world (microcosm) and its source (macrocosm). Therefore, gimel represents a *uniting intelligence*. Looking beneath the surface causes a word to magically come alive with richer, deeper meaning.

We lose power when we take our language for granted and assume we know what someone really means, when in fact we've seen or heard only the tip of the iceberg. Let's explore questions that you can use to go beneath the surface and more clearly understand another's map of the world.

META-MODEL: DECODE DEEP EXPERIENCE

If you want to achieve authentic understanding in a conversation, the meta-model will help you. Imagine using your language to naturally uncover the deeper meaning of what someone is attempting to convey. The meta-model is a series of questions designed to gather information that was deleted or distorted in the process of communicating. This was NLP's first formal model, published in 1975.

Consider this example. Once, while sitting in the park, I overheard a conversation between a teenager and her father. Her arms folded, her tone curt, she said, "You don't understand me!" The dad, who was noticeably shaken up, communicated defensively, saying: "Nothing I do is ever good enough for you." Needless to say, they were launching words at each other, but there was no real understanding. What if the dad used the meta-model? He could say, "Honey, how do you mean? . . . I want to understand. How will you know when I understand you? . . . What specifically does 'understanding' mean to you?" By asking these questions in a caring tone and listening sincerely, he would uncover more information about his daughter's map of the world so he could speak to her listening style and create understanding.

Meta-model questions include:

- *How so?*
- *How do you know?*

- *What do you mean?*
- *Where specifically?*
- *According to whom?*
- *What specifically do you mean by* _____?
- *What do you see in your mind when you say* _____?

Because these questions penetrate beneath the surface, it is important to establish rapport before using the meta-model. Without rapport these questions may appear invasive. Be sensitive to how your queries are received. You don't want to grill someone with a chain of questions. That'll break rapport! Words have the power to hurt and confuse. Therefore, it's wise to soften your energy with the use of linguistic softeners: *I'm wondering (how do you know?)*, or *I'm curious (how do you mean?)*, or *Please share (what specifically do you see in your mind when you say* _____?). Notice the response you get. This requires *sensory acuity*, the ability to tune in to subtle distinctions.

Brilliant communicators notice subtle changes in the person they are interacting with. Does the person lean forward or pull back? Does her breathing get deeper or shallower? How does her skin color and tonus change? You should see eye movements as the person accesses different parts of the brain to retrieve the information you are requesting. When you pay attention you are able to enter another's map of the world.

VISUAL, AUDITORY, AND KINESTHETIC

NLP says, "Communication is redundant," which means that by nature we are continually communicating. You can more clearly understand someone's map of the world by paying attention to the words they choose. Visual people tend to make pictures in their mind and choose words like "show me" or "paint me a picture." Those who are more visual tend to look up, whereas people who are more auditory look side-to-side more. Auditory people talk to themselves quite often. They use words like "tell me" or "are you hearing what I'm saying." Those who are likely to consider feelings when communicating are more kinesthetic. They tend to look down more often and choose phrases like "I can feel it" or "I'll handle this." Most people are a combination of two or all three. Although a person's choice of wording may appear trivial on the surface, it illuminates how a person is processing information and reveals the deeper structure of their mental map. In other words, by listening to the words people choose you can discern how they code their memories and visions using pictures, sounds, and/or feelings.

We've mentioned the term "listening style" a couple of times. So let's explore the relationship between our speaking and listening styles.

LITERAL AND INFERENTIAL SPEAKING AND LISTENING STYLES

Some people, by their very nature, tend to communicate more literally, others more inferentially. In NLP this tendency to communicate literally or inferentially is a "metaprogram." It's one of the mental filters that determine how a person processes information and perceives the world around them. Metaprograms are context specific; that is, in some contexts a person might generally speak and/or listen more literally. In other contexts, that same person might speak and/or listen more inferentially. Let's look at a few of the ways this tendency can manifest:

- *Literal speaking:* Literal speakers will tell you in no uncertain terms what they are thinking and what they want. They give specific, direct instruction.
- *Inferential speaking:* Inferential speakers will infer things in their speech without saying it directly. They may beat around the bush, giving you hints or clues, expecting you to read between the lines and understand what they want or mean.
- *Literal listening:* Literal listeners need things spelled out; they won't tune in to metaphors, allegory, or subtle cues. They need communication to be clear and unequivocal if they are to comprehend.
- *Inferential listening:* Inferential listeners infer things from what someone else says and take action without being asked. They read between the lines and pick up on subtle cues.

Let me illustrate this. Imagine we know a couple in a relationship. The woman has a metaprogram in the context of intimacy to communicate inferentially—she expects her man to know what she wants and read between the lines. As she's curled up on the couch in her nightie under a blanket, she says to her lover, "Gosh, it's really cold in here." What she really means, when we look beneath the surface of her words, is: "Honey, would you please start the fireplace and come snuggle with me?" If her man's metaprogram, in this context, is to listen literally, then he might hear the statement and reply, "Yes, it is cold." Or maybe he wouldn't say anything at all because in his mind there was nothing in that sentence requiring a response. He interpreted it as a statement of fact. In the absence of Supreme Influence, the woman could project all kinds of disempowering meanings on the man and this experience—*He's so inconsiderate! Why can't he see that I'm asking for some love and romance!* Perhaps she gets quiet and withdraws. The man thinks, *What happened? I have no idea why she suddenly got so upset! Everything was fine just a moment ago.* In this situation, the meta-model can be a powerful tool for clear communication. The man can recognize there is a piece of information he somehow missed and respond differently, "Darling, I would love to know specifically what you would like from me. I would love to bring you happiness right now." The woman can recognize he is asking for literal communication and respond accordingly, "I would love you to light the fire and hold me close right now." Now the communication gap has been bridged.

It's wise to determine if people's speaking and listening styles are more literal or inferential, because then you can tailor your communication to speak into their listening. Pay attention to the words they choose. Are they using straightforward or flowery language? Are they matter-of-fact or artfully vague? Do they act on subtle cues or wait for direct commands? How about you? Do you tend to speak and listen more literally or inferentially? Remember, styles are context specific, but now that you're aware these differences exist, you have more resources to communicate effectively. You can use your language to elicit the deeper meaning beyond words—the pictures, sounds, and feelings in your own and others' innermost beings.

PERCEPTION IS PROJECTION

*If the doors of perception were cleansed every
thing would appear to man as it is: infinite.*

—WILLIAM BLAKE

Once while walking in New York City, I looked up at the
Empire State Building and was moved with a sense of awe.
I loved it for what it was, a marvel of human ingenuity. I've
come to understand that when I see a building like that, well,
I see with my eyes. When an architect looks at a skyscraper,
her eye will pick up information mine will not. She will have
an appreciation and recognition of the materials used, the
design lineage, the time involved from conception to comple-
tion, the physics of space, and the history and evolution of
skyscrapers. When an office worker looks at a skyscraper, he
might see himself going to work and punching a clock. He
sees the space in which he does his job. What do you see when
you look at the marvels of the world? What do you see when
you look at other people? The depth of perspective you have
and the meaning you give to things do not reflect the incal-
culable array of objective possibilities as much as they reflect
your own mental landscapes.

This chapter is about self-awareness. It's about waking up to the realization that what you perceive in others, and the world around you, reflects something about you. Perception is not reality; perception is projection. You do not see reality directly; rather, you perceive your own experience of reality mapped onto the world around you.

Here's a little "perception is projection" scenario.

Suppose four women are having lunch together in a restaurant and a man passes their table. One woman didn't notice the man. The second woman says aloud, "He looks sexy and wealthy. He's probably taken." The third woman says, "I don't know about that. I think there's something about him you just can't trust." The fourth woman says, "Hush! You don't want him to know we're talking about him!" What's going on here? Each woman sees something different based on her map of the world. What they see (or don't see!) in the man isn't necessarily about him. Their perceptions are filtered through the frames in their own mind. Perhaps the woman who is suspicious may have felt jilted in a past relationship, and the man triggered her memory. If so, she may have developed a belief regarding whom she can and cannot trust. She unconsciously projects this belief, which influences how she perceives the universe. This woman's subjective experience colors the objective reality that a man walked by the table.

Suppose Mother Teresa or a saint or a bodhisattva was sitting at the table and saw the same man. She'd probably see the divine, as she would in all people passing by.

Everyone looks through the lens of his or her own consciousness.

What you notice in others—the things you love and the things that charge and excite you—are a clue to your own map. Think about how many people you simply pass without second thought, while others capture your attention. What's the difference between the people who fade into the background and the ones who pop into your awareness? It's not just about the other person. What you notice is mirroring something back to you—about you. Anytime someone sparks an intense response in you, something within you is being reflected in the mirror of that person. Carl Jung said, "Everything that irritates us about others can lead us to an understanding of ourselves."

To different minds, the same world
is a hell, and a heaven.
—RALPH WALDO EMERSON

Let's say someone says or does something, and you unconsciously react. If so, your response is not about the other person. When you squeeze an orange, what do you get? You don't get grape juice, you get *orange* juice—you get what's inside. Similarly, when you're squeezed by what appears to be the pressures of life, what comes out of you is what's inside. Whatever it is, honor it, and get curious about it. Ask, "What is the gift here?" Write your answers in your journal.

Have you ever been in a situation where something happened and you got mentally or emotionally worked up about it? Perhaps you were certain you were right and the other person was wrong, only to discover later that you had misunderstood.

Your interpretation of your perception was off, and so you projected all sorts of meaning. Oops!

You create your experience based on what you focus on and the meaning you assign to things. No two human beings share the same observations—or experiences. Here's a story that illustrates this:

A dear friend of mine grew up in profoundly challenging family circumstances. He never met his father, and his mother was addicted to drugs. My friend, his older brother, and their younger sister struggled to survive their early years. Despite his chaotic childhood, my friend created a prosperous life. He's an honorable family man who is spiritually centered, has built successful businesses and wealth, and enjoys wellness and authentic relationships. He contributes to causes he believes in and played professional football, which was one of his lifelong dreams. His siblings' lives reflect different stories. His brother spent time in prison. His sister died from a drug overdose, leaving two young children behind. One day my friend visited his brother in the penitentiary and asked, "What brought you to this?" His brother replied, "With a mom and dad like ours, what else could you expect?"

When my friend told me this story over dinner, I asked him, "What do you believe has brought you to where you are in life?"

He smiled and said, "With a mom and dad like mine, what else could you expect?"

Tony Robbins once said to me, "It's not what happens to you in life that makes the difference; it's what you focus on, and the meaning you give to things, that shapes your destiny." My friend harnessed the energy of his childhood experience and channeled it. The very circumstances that crushed his brother's spirit motivated my friend to create a rich life.

Seek not to change the world, but choose
to change your mind about the world.

—A COURSE IN MIRACLES

THE MEANING OF MEANING:
YOU ARE MAKING IT UP!

Here's a secret taught by ancient wisdom traditions and enlightened masters.

Ready? *You're making it up!*

Through your intention, observation, and declaration, you create your experience of reality from one moment to the next. Out of infinite possibilities, you have endless ways to perceive. Because what you see has everything to do with what you focus on and the meaning you assign to your experiences, it makes sense to consciously choose empowering meanings that uplift.

Here's a parable.

There once was an old man who sat outside the walls of a great city. When travelers approached, they would ask, "What kinds of people live in this city?" The old man would answer, "What kind of people live in the place where you came from?" If the travelers answered, "Only bad people live in the place where we came from," the old man would reply, "Continue on. You will only find bad people here." But if the travelers answered, "Good people live in the place where we came from," then the old man would say, "Enter, for here too you will find good people."

Nothing is either good or bad,
but thinking makes it so.

—HAMLET, WILLIAM SHAKESPEARE

Great teachers teach us that we do not see the world as it is; rather, we see the world as we are. As my dear friend Michael Beckwith says, "You do not describe what you see, you see what you describe." The wise old man in the folk tale knew people have a tendency to respond based on past experiences and expectations—until they wake up.

Or to state this scientifically: neurological associations in the brain cause us to repeatedly look for what we have always seen, even though the situation before us is new. The great news is you have the power to transform neuroassociations that no longer serve you into neuroassociations that do!

RETICULAR ACTIVATING SYSTEM (RAS)

A structure in the human brain stem, known as the reticular cortex, is responsible for an autonomic response referred to as the *reticular activating system* (RAS). In simple terms, the RAS alerts you to important information. It tells you what to notice. The RAS filters out irrelevant data, telling you what is worth paying attention to. Here's what is newsworthy: you can program the RAS to focus on your vision.

Have you ever purchased a car you thought was unique and different, but the moment you drove it off the lot you began to notice a shocking number of nearly identical cars on the road? Those cars were there previously, but you didn't see them because they had no meaning for you. Once you bought *your* car, you programmed your RAS to notice similar vehicles.

The RAS exists in a primitive portion of your brain that regulates states of consciousness, from sleep to alertness, and is also involved in the body's fight-or-flight response. You can imagine how in caveman days, anytime danger lurked the RAS would pick up on the danger and stimulate a release of adrenaline to energize the caveman's response. As we evolved as humans, this part of the brain developed beyond a basic survival mechanism. Researchers have linked the RAS to motivation, because when the RAS is stimulated, a person becomes more awake and active.

The RAS's neural connections are essential to processing information and learning. Your conscious mind focuses on small chunks of information at a time. The RAS is an unconscious process that causes you to notice information that matches your dominant thoughts and beliefs.

Through language, you can purposefully program your RAS to pay attention to information that will support you in accomplishing your mission. For instance, you are learning to wisely direct your RAS as you read this book! This will help you achieve your goals by alerting you to possibilities you might previously have overlooked.

PERCEPTION CAN ACTIVATE BRILLIANCE

What you look for in the world influences what materializes. What you perceive in the people around you influences how they show up. Have you ever expected someone to screw up, and then they did? How about the opposite—has someone ever believed in you even more than you believed in yourself at the time? Someone who saw your magnificence, and through their reflection you remembered your creative powers.

Many moons ago, someone saw my brilliance at a time when I felt dark and dim. I had dropped out of my senior year of high school with a 1.6 grade point average, and I felt like a loser. Determined to create a life that worked, I decided to take my high school equivalency test and earn my certificate. Then I enrolled in community college before my peers had finished high school. One day during my first semester, my English professor, an eccentric Yale graduate with a wild mane of mad-scientist hair, asked me to stay after class. "Oh no," I thought. "What have I done this time?" I had flashbacks of spending countless hours in after-school detention. But Dr. Bredenberg surprised me. He said, "Niurka, you are brilliant. You should not be in this class. You should be in the honors class." With that, he sent me to the dean.

The dean and I connected. He said, "We are inviting you to join our honors program on Dr. Bredenberg's recommendation, which means we will pay your tuition." I could hardly believe my ears! I sat silently ecstatic and did my best not to fly out of my seat and tackle him with a hug. At the time I was working two jobs to cover the basics and pay for school. Then the dean said, "The only requirement is that you maintain a minimum 3.5 grade point average." For a moment, my heart sank—3.5? But Dr. Bredenberg's belief in me reminded me of a belief I had deep down—I am smart!

I could see myself in Dr. Bredenberg's reflection. His observation activated the qualities of *brilliance* in me. He evoked my genius. He knew it was there, and because he knew it, I looked for it. I appreciated him for seeing *me*, and I was determined to prove him right.

I focused on my schoolwork and grades. At the end of my first semester I had earned a perfect 4.0. The next semester I earned another 4.0, and then again in the following semester. My self-perception started changing. I began to think, "Maybe I'm not that high school dropout who gets in trouble and does bad things. Maybe I am brilliant! Maybe I *can* do anything I want to do and be anyone I *want* to be."

As my identity shifted, so did my projections. And the girl who hated elementary school and was jaded in junior high now was seeing academics through a new lens. I began enjoying school, a miracle in itself. I became vice president of finance for an honors fraternity, won academic awards, became student body president, started a sorority, and cultivated confidence.

In less than a year, I had created a new reality. I was a new person in a new realm. My life was forever changed. The defining moment that sparked my transformation was one person's clear and present observation.

It's kind of fun to do the impossible.

—WALT DISNEY

This phenomenon of transformative expectation has been documented. Robert Rosenthal and Lenore Jacobson refer to it as the Pygmalion effect. In 1968 researchers created an experiment using elementary school teachers. Certain teachers were given a classroom of students and told the students had low

IQs. Other teachers were given a classroom of supposedly gifted children. The results clearly showed that *teacher expectations influence student performance.* Positive expectations influenced performance positively. Negative expectations influenced performance negatively. "When we expect certain behaviors of others, we act in ways that make the expected behavior more likely to occur," Rosenthal summarized in 1985.

You too have the power to bring out the best in every person you encounter. Imagine what happens to our collective journey as we actively see genius in our children, in one another, and in ourselves.

At times our own light goes out and is rekindled
by a spark from another person. Each of us
has cause to think with deep
gratitude of those who have lighted
the flame within us.
—ALBERT SCHWEITZER

Here is a Supreme Influence practice to activate genius:

Encourage others. Catch people doing things right. Recognize yourself doing things right. Honor children for being and also for doing things well. Have you noticed how a child behaves differently for different adults? In the presence of a certain adult, the child may act out with poor behavior. In the presence of another adult, that same child will be conscientious, curious, and kind. What's different? The child is matching each adult's vibe and expectations.

Each second we live is a new and unique
moment of the universe, a moment that will
never be again. And what do we teach our
children? We teach them that two and two make
four, and that Paris is the capital of France.
When will we also teach them what they are?
We should say to each of them: Do you know
what you are? You are a marvel. You are unique.
In all the years that have passed, there has never
been another child like you. Your legs, your
arms, your clever fingers, the way you move. You
may become a Shakespeare, a Michelangelo, a
Beethoven. You have the capacity for anything.
Yes, you are a marvel.

—PABLO PICASSO

What lessons can we learn from this? Give your lover praise.
Let your friends know how much you appreciate them. Follow
Benjamin Franklin's suggestion, "Speak ill of no man, but speak
all the good you know of everybody." Honor your team members
for their contributions. Recognize each person's Supreme Influence. In the corporate world, this is akin to *leading by strengths*.
Everyone has a gift. A leader knows how to evoke them.

The more you practice conscious awareness, the clearer your
perceptions become. You enter a neutral space not swayed by
anything outside of you.

8

CHOOSE WORDS WISELY

Language is a process of free creation;
its laws and principles are fixed,
but the manner in which the principles of
generation are used is free and infinitely varied.
Even the interpretation and use of words involves a
process of free creation.

—NOAM CHOMSKY

When you open your mouth to speak, how many possible combinations of words and expressions could come out? Infinite! There are limitless ways to describe the human experience. You have choice. Therefore, enjoy the process of free creation. Learn how to wield your language gracefully and masterfully, like a virtuoso violinist who translates what is in his heart and mind into notes and makes music that elevates us all. You too have a song. What melody does your heart long to sing? How can you translate your melody into elegant and wise words that inspire action in yourself and others? This chapter will magnify the hidden power of words. It will shed light on how language announces what a person believes, and it will show you how to enrich every area of life by choosing words wisely.

Language is the inventory of human experience.

—L.W. LOCKHART

Language reveals one's consciousness. Every statement you make and every question you ask contain *embedded assumptions* that reveal your values, attitudes, and worldview. Let's get curious. What has your language been revealing about you? If you were to walk around with a voice recorder for a day (or better yet, if you could put a recorder in your brain!), what would you hear when you touched playback? Would your thoughts and words express appreciation and encouragement? Would your tone emanate authenticity, honor, and kindness? Or would the recording capture you looping thoughts about problems, focusing on the past, bringing up doubts, perhaps even speaking unkindly of others or even yourself? Throughout the day, would you contradict—or champion—your self and your vision?

What if you knew that *you create as you speak?* Your words have that much power! When you speak, your language *assumes* the existence of something that illuminates your map of reality and summons what you declare. In other words, language contains *presuppositions.* Let's look at the word *presupposition* a little deeper. The prefix *pre-* means "to come before." The word *suppose* corresponds to *supposition,* which means something "believed to be true." *Suppose* stems from the Latin verb *supponere,* which means "to place under." Therefore, the presuppositions in language are *sub,* meaning *under* the conscious mind. They can emerge outside of your conscious awareness, *yet* they influence *everything* in your life. So let's bring them to the surface. Let's magnify these embedded assumptions in language, so that you may consciously choose words that match your intent.

Examine the presuppositions, the embedded assumptions, in this sentence:

You are becoming even more aware of the vast amount of information you convey about your attitudes and beliefs through your language.

In the sentence above, I used the words "you are becoming even more aware." What are the embedded assumptions in this statement? In other words, what information or relationships must be accepted as truth to make sense of what's being said? Before you answer, notice the subtle differences between the sentences below:

1. You are not aware.
2. Most people are not aware.
3. You may not be aware.
4. You may not yet be aware.
5. You are becoming aware.
6. You arc becoming even more aware.

I could have used any one of the sentences above to convey what may appear to be a similar meaning, but which sentence offers the most empowering possibility?

- Sentence 1 gives no hope and no credit to the reader.
- Sentence 2 offers the reader a little personal hope, but it makes a sweeping generalization and offers little hope for humanity.
- Sentence 3 suggests you could be aware, but assumes you're likely not.

- Sentence 4 assumes that if you're not aware, it's quite possible you will be.
- Sentence 5 frames possibility and creates the space for you to be aware right now! You have just expanded.
- Sentence 6 infers that you are presently aware and are becoming more so, which invites your brain to move in that direction.

Look at those sentences again. They are different from one another by only a few words! The shift in words is subtle, but the difference in the meaning communicated is *huge*! This is the level of subtlety and distinction you are learning and mastering along our journey together. One word can make a difference.

This is especially important in positions of leadership. When a leader speaks, an undiscerning listener may be unconsciously influenced to accept the leader's words as truth. Imagine if a business expert-mentor whom people admire said, "Most people who start their own business fail because they don't have the right systems in place." Will that statement empower those who listen? Well, if you were a start-up entrepreneur, you might think that it's wise to know what doesn't work so you can focus on what does. But considering that we live in a universe of infinite possibility, and that our language has power to create and destroy, is this choice of language the wisest one to speak into existence? What if the leader said instead: "As you implement proven systems into your business and continually refine them, you create the conditions to achieve your goals." Notice how this sentence gives the listener affirmative direction.

LET'S GET REAL: AUTHENTICITY IS POWER

Supreme Influence is grounded in speaking *your* truth. It's not about using flowery language or euphemisms to mask or suppress difficult experiences. It's not about fooling yourself into thinking things are okay when they're not. Supreme Influence is about being real with what *is*, facing it head-on and not looking away, and then using thoughts and language to shape an elevated reality.

The dictionary defines *euphemism* as the act of substituting a mild, indirect, or vague term for one considered harsh or offensive. For example, when the military accidentally kills one of its troops, the death is attributed to "friendly fire." That term is a euphemism. An unpleasant situation has been stamped with a pretty label intended to disguise its unpleasantness and to make it sound agreeable. The euphemism presents the tragedy in a benign way that sounds socially acceptable, and thus people do not challenge it.

Speaking in euphemisms is *not* what is being proposed here.

I'm suggesting something evolutionary. Rather than changing the label, look through what currently *is* into what could be. Focus on transforming problems into possibilities by imagining what you want in your mind. Then use language to call forth the experiences you envision. In every situation you'll find elements of light and dark, yin and yang. Where is your focus being directed? You can consciously choose more accurate and empowering words to describe any situation. Let's explore how.

LANGUAGE: A PORTAL INTO THE MIND

A little earlier we spoke of the recorder that might capture your choice of words throughout the day. Consider those word choices. What words and phrases have you been regularly using, and what insights can you gain from them? Observe your language as if you were an anthropologist . . . from Pluto. Notice words that you tend to use often. Write them down in your journal. Reflect. Without judgment, ask yourself, what do these words evoke within me? How do they make me feel? You can also set reminders for yourself. For example, schedule your cell phone to chime a message at certain times of the day—"What are you speaking into existence right now?" or "Be present to the language you choose" or "Breathe, be still, and listen to your own inner guidance." Have fun with it! Pick fanciful times like 11:11, 1:11, 3:33, 5:55, etc. You could use a ringtone that ignites your fire, like the theme from *Rocky*, or one that calms your being, like Tibetan bells—whatever you like. This daily ritual will stimulate you to be more aware of the language you use and empower you to choose words wisely.

A powerful agent is the right word. Whenever we come upon one of those intensely right words . . . the resulting effect is physical as well as spiritual, and electrically prompt.

—MARK TWAIN

Language is a portal into the mind. It will reveal if someone perceives the world through the lens of . . .

Problem: This will never work.
Or
Possibility: There's always a way.

Fear: I'm not falling in love again because it's a recipe for pain.

Or

Love: The more love I give, the more love I feel. Love is all around me.

Scarcity: It's too expensive. I can't afford it.

Or

Abundance: I appreciate and am grateful for the blessings in my life.

Confusion: I don't understand how he could do that.

Or

Clarity: I understand there are multiple ways to perceive this situation.

Struggle: Life is hard, and then you die.

Or

Allowing: There is a gift in every moment.

Neediness: I need help. I can't do it.

Or

Resourcefulness: I have unlimited resources within me and surrounding me.

Separation: I'm alone.

Or

Unity: The same life force that beats my heart is beating your heart right now.

Examine the list above and compare it to the language you've been using. Look at the notes you wrote in your journal and ask yourself, "Have I been perceiving the world through the lens of problem or possibility, fear or love, scarcity or abundance, confusion or clarity, struggle or allowing, neediness or resourcefulness, separation or unity?" Awareness is the first step to conscious transformation. With awareness, you can discipline your language and condition yourself to speak in a way that produces desirable results and inspires others in the process. When you elevate your language, you elevate every area of your life. This is not merely *positive thinking*. This is using your language to rewire your brain and to discover the gift in each moment.

PRESUPPOSITIONS AND MIND READS

We've been exploring *your* language. Now let's study what you hear in the language of others. When you observe others and listen to them speak, be aware of what is being presupposed. It's essential to recognize the difference between presuppositions embedded in language and assuming you know what someone is thinking. The latter is known as a *mind read*.

A mind read is something inferred or deduced from language but not actually stated. Because it is not stated, we cannot accurately assume what is meant. You can use the meta-model discussed in chapter 6 to gather more information, which then enables you to avoid inaccurately mind reading another's experience. With the meta-model, you ask questions like *how so, what,* or *who specifically* so that you elicit deeper meaning. This allows you to discern if you are picking up accurate information. Remember to be in rapport with the other person when using the meta-model; otherwise the questions can come across as abrasive.

Let's illuminate the distinctions between presuppositions and mind reads by considering the statements below.

Statement: This is the last time she's going to agree to that.

Mind read: She's been pushed to her limits. She's making compromises. She's upset.

Presupposition: 1. There is a time.

           2. She agreed to something before.

           3. She is going to agree.

           4. There is something to agree to.

Statement: He's always smiling when he sees me.

Mind read: He's a happy man. I make him smile. He has a crush on me.

Presupposition: 1. He smiles.

           2. He sees me.

Statement: It's better now that we're here together.

Mind read: It wasn't good before. Being together is better than being alone. They missed each other.

Presupposition: 1. We're together now.

           2. There is a comparison being made.

Statement: I always talk to my husband when I make decisions.

Mind read: They make mutual decisions. She's a weak woman who can't make her own decisions.

Presupposition: 1. I have a husband.

           2. I talk to my husband.

           3. I make decisions.

Each of these mind reads *may* be an accurate reflection of the person's internal representation, but it's difficult to discern without more information. Sometimes you can mind read and be correct; at other times, mind reading leaves room for interpretation and mistakes. Communication is layered in nuance. Sometimes it's essential to mind read—to read between the lines. Other times it makes more sense to ask questions to gain clarity. Either way, brilliant communicators recognize the subtle distinction between what is said and what could be assumed.

Now let's play with language and consider how our perception and actions are influenced by the words we choose.

PLAY WITH LANGUAGE TO EXPAND POSSIBILITY

I'm going to give you two sentences. Notice the experience each one evokes—what images you conjure and how they make you feel.

- I'm just a mom.
- I am a present, loving presence in my family's lives. I am the queen mother.

Now, you may be thinking, "Yeah, right, Niurka! Obviously the second sentence is much more inspiring, but nobody talks like that! And if they did, you'd think they were a bit dramatic or at least incredibly verbose!" Yes, it may seem a little unusual at first. You've been talking most of your life and probably have never been so conscious of what you're saying. But what if you knew that by choosing your words more precisely, everything in your life would improve? Wouldn't it make sense to get a little playful and explore the potential your language possesses to create your ultimate dream life?

You will *move toward* what you focus on; you will experience what you declare.

Let's spice up our language to stretch the boundaries of what's possible. We can always refine or tone down our language later to craft sentences that sound more usual to you. But right now, I encourage you to play! Some of this language may sound a little foreign at first, because we've all been conditioned to speak in certain ways. But it's this kind of extraordinary thinking that is genius—*it's evolutionary!* When I talk with people, my language often surprises them. But soon they mirror me and use many of the same dynamic words of power. This new way of using words uplifts their life and activates their creative intelligence.

Let's return to the example of "I'm just a mom" in contrast to "I am a present, loving presence in my family's lives. I am the queen mother." Notice the pictures, sounds, and feelings each statement evokes. What's the difference? Which one calls forth greater grace, power, and love? When a mother declares the second statement confidence exudes from every cell in her being. Her presence is felt. If she previously thought she was "just a mom," she now finds herself expanding the spectrum of her self-perception. She realizes she is not bound by any single, static identity. She has choice. As her consciousness expands to include other dimensions of *self*, people in her life begin seeing her as expansively as she sees herself. Maybe a woman reading this is thinking, "I don't know if that's true for me. I've never thought of myself as a queen mother." If it sounds a bit outrageous, that's okay.

Think like a queen. A queen is not afraid to fail.
Failure is another stepping-stone to greatness.
—OPRAH WINFREY

In the next few chapters, we'll explore how you can wield language in a way that resonates, inspiring you to create a life you love, one brimming with adventure and shared successes . . . even if that life has seemed a bit out of reach in the past.

As you choose empowering language, you consciously re-invent yourself. Invest a moment right now, and consciously craft one "I am" statement. Before you write it down, say the statement in your mind and tune in to your body to ensure it feels good. Then write it down in your journal. Be creative and choose potent, life-affirming words.

I am _____.

Now, look at what you wrote, and declare it so. As you consciously choose your thoughts and words, you elevate everyone and everything around you. Thoughts and words are the foundation on which we create our world.

THE POWER TO NAME

One of the greatest powers you have is the power to name. In the story of Genesis, God gives man the authority to name each living creature. People, brands, things, and experiences tend to live up to their name. In ancient times, a name not only stood for a person; it represented their honor, character, and life's work. Even symbols or crests were associated with family names. Some individuals who experienced profound awakenings changed their names to reflect their new sense of self. Muhammad Ali, the great boxer, philanthropist, and social activist, was born Cassius Marcellus Clay Jr. When asked in a press conference why he changed his name, Ali said, "*Muhammad* means one who's worthy of all praises and one who's praiseworthy, and *Ali* means the most high. But *Clay* only meant dirt with no ingredients. . . . Cassius Clay was the name of the white slave master . . . and I am free." Ali knew that names are linked to identity. He declared himself "the Greatest," and he has lived up to his name. Therefore, consciously name your children, companies, projects, and endeavors with care. Choose names that not only sound pleasing but that reflect your authentic aims.

I am the greatest.
I said that even before I knew I was.

—MUHAMMAD ALI

SOMETHING TO CONSIDER AS
WE EVOLVE OUR WORLD

The power to name things influences societies, nations, and collective realities. In a moment we will shine a light on the embedded assumptions in the names, titles, and missions of a few social causes and organizations. As we do, please keep an open mind. Consider the choice of wording. Does it inspire affirmative action toward a clear vision? Or does it push away from something unwanted? Get curious. Since we have infinite potential combinations of words and phrases, doesn't it make sense to consciously craft titles that inspire action toward a desired aim?

This book affirms that we are creators and that the names we assign to our projects, products, and organizations influence our perception, focus, and overall sense of direction. I am proposing that our individual and collective reality will improve when each one of us chooses to name our most cherished creations with full conscious intent. As we actively choose our words wisely, we elevate what shows up in our lives. We cannot evolve our world by speaking in the present the way we have spoken in the past.

The people who are crazy enough
to think they can change the world
are the ones who do.

—STEVE JOBS

Look at the social causes below. Say each name out loud, one at a time. Notice how each term resonates in your body. These examples will magnify the point about how language influences our collective reality.

- War on Drugs
- Big Brothers Big Sisters
- Disease prevention
- Anti-aging
- Museum of Tolerance
- United Nations

First, let me be clear. I honor the individuals supporting these causes. I recognize the ambition to serve humanity. But perhaps (for some of these examples) there may be a more empowering way of formulating language, directing energy, and achieving the ultimate goal. Also, this discussion is in no way meant to negate anyone's experience. Yes, drug addiction and abuse do cause harm. Disease and intolerance can affect people. Acknowledging these can be very real experiences. How can we create empowering solutions that alchemize these circumstances? One thing we can do is direct our attention and language toward what is wanted rather than pushing away from what is unwanted.

Okay . . . let's go a little deeper.

War on Drugs

What does the war on drugs aim to accomplish? Is the intention really to engage in war? "War" is a concept most would agree is as insidious and destructive as drug abuse, right? Notice the ambiguity of the initiative's name. Based on the wording, it's unclear if this cause advocates for a war against drugs or if it implies the war itself is "on drugs." Four-plus decades after President Nixon declared the "war on drugs," this terminology is still prevalent, even though the Global Commission on Drug Policy has stated, "The global war on drugs has failed." Fortunately, in 2009 the Obama administration decided to no longer use the term, declaring it "counterproductive."

I would hope that the highest intent of this campaign is to educate people to be empowered, healthy, and able to make wise choices. When this aim is the focus, the problem is circumnavigated. If a person is empowered, healthy, and making wise choices, it logically follows that drug abuse will not become a problem. It's likely not even relevant.

In schools across the United States, children participate in National Red Ribbon Week to demonstrate their support for a drug-free America. Nearly 80 percent of U.S. school districts teach a curriculum called DARE, which is an acronym for Drug Abuse Resistance Education. It's an initiative aimed at educating children. However, education about *resisting* abuse is different from education about *choosing* healthy choices.

Additionally, notice the ambiguity with the word *drug*. In the United States, we have a governmental agency called the Food and Drug Administration that regulates food and pharmaceuticals. Therefore, we have one governmental policy fighting drugs and another agency approving drugs. Without clear distinctions in language to point the way, how is a child to know which drugs are sanctioned and which drugs are condemned? And isn't it interesting that food and drugs are overseen by the same agency?

Currently in the United States, we have many causes, which at their deepest level have noble intentions, but the language used keeps energies polarized, which perpetuates battle. For example, we have a "war on terror," a "war on poverty," a "fight against cancer," and a "fight against obesity." Mother Teresa knew that fighting something actually fuels it. She said, "I was once asked why I don't participate in antiwar demonstrations. I said that I will never do that, but as soon as you have a pro-peace rally, I'll be there."

Choosing language wisely is an important step in improving our lives and our world. Please realize this is *not* just changing words. It's shifting our concentration toward a worthwhile direction rather than pushing away from past problems.

Blessed are the peacemakers,
for they shall be called children of God.

—MATTHEW 5:9

In contrast, let's explore another name.

Big Brothers Big Sisters

Big Brothers Big Sisters states their vision as "all children achieve success in life." Consider how the choice in language directs attention toward a desired aim. For more than one hundred years, Big Brothers Big Sisters have been living up to their name and helping children realize their potential by matching them with adult role models ("Bigs"). They focus on developing meaningful, nurturing relationships that have a positive and lasting influence on the lives of young people. Researchers found that after eighteen months of spending time with their "Bigs," the little brothers and sisters were 46 percent less likely to begin using illegal drugs, compared to children who were not in the program. Contrast these results to DARE, which has been called an "ineffective program" by the U.S. Surgeon General.

Here's another example.

Disease Prevention

We have a federal agency called the Centers for Disease Control and Prevention. Consider the language. The word *disease* can be broken down into *dis-*, which is a negation, and *ease*. Therefore, disease is the negation of ease. Certainly, diseases have affected people, but if the focus is on controlling or preventing the negation of ease versus moving toward health and well-being, then disease is more likely to manifest.

Let's look at the word *prevention*. Is the energy focused toward what is wanted or away from what is not wanted? Which is more empowering, promoting health or preventing disease? Are they the same thing?

Without awareness of the hidden power of words, these two ideas can seem interchangeable. But are they really? Some may think they're slightly different yet compatible; maybe it's a good idea to focus on both—promoting health and preventing disease. Possibly, but because disease can only thrive in a willing host body, if a person's body is consistently healthy, it's possible disease prevention may not be necessary. Now, I'm not a doctor, and I'm certainly not making any health claims. This does not replace the advice of a health-care provider. But isn't it interesting how shifting language shifts an entire focus? How have you been communicating with your body? Do you think your body would respond differently to preventing disease versus promoting health? How does promoting health differ from embodying health or even radiating health? The word *promoting* can imply health is absent whereas *embodying* implies it's present, and *radiating* health implies not only is health present, it's expansive! What if we not only radiated health but also relished in the magnificence of Supreme health? What if we had a government agency called the Centers for Supreme Health and Well-being? How would the shift in language change our cultural priorities? Sure, what I'm saying may seem controversial, but it represents a fundamental shift in our values. Through conscious communication, we form the infrastructure from which we build our world.

Let's look at another example.

Anti-aging

What is the presupposition in the anti-aging movement? *Anti* means "against." Therefore, there's resistance against aging. Certainly we all want to be in excellent health, and it's possible to radiate health in our advanced years. Anti-aging emphasizes the virtues of youth and beauty (of which there are many) while minimizing the virtues of age. Aging is a natural process. It's important to acknowledge the merits that come with every stage of life. As many indigenous cultures realize, age can be a symbol of wisdom—lifetimes of integrated knowledge—rather than something to run from or resist. Instead of focusing on anti-aging, we could focus on being healthy and vibrant at any age.

One of my dear friends is an anti-aging expert. I shared my thoughts about the concept of "anti-aging" and he agreed the term was up for a face-lift. Yet he and I had vastly different IRs of what the term meant. When I think of aging, I see myself as a wise old crone with long gray hair meditating in my garden, creating art, surrounded by young people who come to me for wisdom. When he thinks of aging, he sees 50-year-olds dying prematurely of heart disease, stroke, cancer, and other preventable illnesses. To him, anti-aging is about "fighting the ravages of aging and saving people from senility, immobility, and premature deaths." The movement's aim is to help people live healthy and strong, to be able bodied and sharp minded until the moment of transition. We agreed that shifting the focus toward what is wanted—health, vitality, and radiant well-being in all stages of life—is a wiser choice.

Museum of Tolerance

What can we discern from the name Museum of Tolerance? Tolerance is definitely an evolution from intolerance and a giant leap toward empowerment from hatred. However, is "tolerance" the ultimate aim? How does tolerance differ from acceptance or honoring our differences? Imagine if groups who thought they would "tolerate" each other instead came to embrace forgiveness, appreciation, or even curiosity? How would that change the experience? It's not just a simple word switch; the words represent an expansion in consciousness. Perhaps in the past *tolerance* was a more accurate word to describe the resolution between groups who had experienced high tension. Maybe the shift to peace was too high a jump. Maybe it's an evolution from tolerance to curiosity to fascination to appreciation to understanding to harmony. Maybe peace isn't necessarily an instant evolution—but it could be.

As we evolve, it is essential that our language evolves. Here is one brilliant example.

United Nations

In 1945, fifty-one countries committed to international peace, promoting social progress, human rights, and improving standards of living for all people, came together and formed the United Nations. This international organization, born from the pain of World War II, is a good example of conscious evolution. Instead of fighting the war, these leaders focused on "developing friendly relation among nations," and their name reflects it. The word *united* means "one" or "oneness." The word *nations* means "born" or "coming into existence." Thus, the name presupposes oneness coming into existence.

LANGUAGE OF POSSIBILITY PAVES THE WAY

Creating our world the way we want it to be, in a way that honors everyone's uniqueness, requires conscious communication. Of course this process involves more than choosing words wisely. It begins by imagining our highest intent *before* we assign it a name and speak it into existence. Our choice in language can influence the thoughts of others, which in turn influences how they appear and act—everything is connected in a unified field. How we choose to name our children, projects, companies, organizations, and causes forms the foundation for our emerging way of life. It is not a simple matter of switching the name of the Centers for Disease Control and Prevention to the Centers for Supreme Health and Well-being. This change is an example of one essential progression. The real power exists not only in the words but in conjunction with the shift in focus, priority, and direction. A new word will conjure a new internal representation and a new manifestation to match.

Through conscious thinking and speaking we can redefine, rename, and recontextualize our companies, communities, nations, and world to better align with the truth of who we are and how we choose to live—in harmony and cooperation. New, carefully crafted words can *create* new worlds. The key is focusing on where we want to go. As Colin Powell once said, "Always focus on the front windshield and not the rearview mirror."

9

DOORS OF OPPORTUNITY

Nature is a masterful teacher when you have the subtle aware-ness to recognize her signs and symbols. I witnessed such a lesson unfold one bright, sunny morning at my local coffee shop. A few minutes before I arrived, a tiny sparrow had flown in and set off a panic among the patrons, who hovered around the frightened bird as it frantically sought freedom through a solid windowpane.

Through the glass, the little bird could see his escape. He mustered his might and, in a fierce attempt at freedom, flew smack into the window. Exhausted and desperate, but with single-minded focus, he summoned his pluck once more. Again he rammed into the window, and his little body collapsed onto the floor.

Apparently this had been going on for several minutes, and no one knew quite what to do. As the people huddled around the little bird, he again resumed his frantic efforts. Meanwhile I noticed a wide-open door just six feet away. The sparrow was running out of fight, and his racing heartbeat was visible through his feathers. A life-or-death tragedy was playing itself out in my local coffee shop! To be free, all this little bird had to do was look around and fly through a wide-open door—freedom was seconds away!

Feeling a wave of compassion, I remembered the times in my past when I had struggled against seemingly impenetrable forces. I'd work long hours, forcing results through sheer determination, the only way I knew how. For years I continued down that path until one day . . . I stopped. Like the sparrow, I was exhausted, close to collapse. I was weary from banging my head against the window, tired of striving, pushing, and pleading. And for what purpose? To what end? I knew life had to be more than just a seeming struggle to survive or get ahead. When I finally paused, took a deep breath, grounded myself, and expanded my aware-ness—a miraculous thing happened. My prayers were answered, often before I even formulated the question. I realized that all along there were *wide-open doors* all around me.

What if you knew with certainty that right now you are sur-rounded by wide-open doors of opportunity? What if you could gracefully walk through the fire of any challenge to the essence of your genuine desires? What if wisdom, understanding, opti-mum health, meaningful relationships, fulfilling purpose, pros-perity, sacred love—anything you can imagine—were a mere mind-set away? This chapter illustrates how doors of opportu-nity surround you and how you can recognize, open, and walk through them.

I have become my own version of an optimist.
If I can't make it through one door,
I'll go through another door—or I'll make a door.
Something terrific will come
no matter how dark the present.
—RABINDRANATH TAGORE

So on that sunny morning, as I watched the sparrow in the coffee shop struggle in its quest for freedom, surrounded by caring but helpless onlookers, I instinctively knew I had the power to transform the situation. My purpose became clear. I summoned a barista and asked for a towel. She quickly reached over the bar, grabbed a small towel, and passed it to me. I scooped up the little creature. Without a word spoken, the patrons cleared a path. The café's chaos transformed into a coordinated rescue dance. I walked with the sparrow to the open door and released it into the sky. The coffee shop erupted in applause. The camaraderie created in that magic moment lifted us all. And for my heroic deed I was bestowed the honor of Coffee Customer of the Week. My picture was taken, and for seven days I enjoyed my favorite drink compliments of the house.

I left the coffee shop that morning inspired, knowing my small actions guided one tiny creature to liberation and simultaneously reminded those present of their Supreme Influence—the ability to summon order in chaos and create harmony in any environment by remaining centered, alert, and ready. Being wholly present and available to the Universe is a key to unlocking your powers. I went in for coffee, but I was prepared for anything.

We all have the means to make a positive difference. How we show up in a coffee shop is as important as how our leaders show up to negotiate international agreements. Small actions matter. In the realms of infinity, there really isn't anything "small" anyway. There is "all" in "small." You can simply smile at someone on the street corner and elevate that person's day with just one gesture. That person may take the sweetness of your reflection home and be kinder with her family and more inspired in her work, influencing everything and everyone she touches. Every moment is sacred, every encounter a miracle. Your presence carries an immeasurable ripple effect.

OPENING INVISIBLE DOORS

Right now, wide-open doors surround you. These doors lead to all the experiences you could possibly desire: freedom, love, courage, happiness, creativity, community, growth, success, adventure, a state of blissful being, or anything else you can imagine. So what keeps them hidden? In Vedantic philosophy there is a term, "maya," which means veils of illusion that create the dream of duality in the manifest universe and can cloud one's vision.

Doors of opportunity remain outside a person's awareness when they are in *reactive consciousness,* which is the tendency to think, speak, and act through the lens of conditioning or programming without present-moment awareness. It's like sleepwalking through life, going through the motions without pausing to *consciously consider* what you are thinking, doing, or saying. Through well-intentioned parents, families, schools, religions, and culture, we have all inherited language and beliefs about what *is* and what is *not* possible. We've even inherited beliefs about who we are. These beliefs influence our choices until we *wake up* and realize we have options.

It is liberating to question the beliefs picked up from childhood—where they come from, are they aligned with our ultimate purpose. Are they even true? Because we will act in accordance with our deepest beliefs (some of which may serve and others may not) until we realize, *we can make the conscious choice to choose* in each moment. Right now, in this moment, we get to determine what to focus on.

Sometimes we stare so long at a door
that is closing that we see too late
the one that is open.

—ALEXANDER GRAHAM BELL

Whatever has or hasn't happened to you up until now is in the past. Tony Robbins once said to me, "The past does not equal the future." What matters most right now is your present-moment energy. You can direct your focus and language to create an amazing life.

Here's a story about being present to the magic of the moment and recognizing doors of opportunity.

AWARE OR AUTOPILOT

One morning while in line at my local café, I noticed the man in front of me. He was hunched over with his arms tightly crossed, breathing heavily and tapping his foot. I patted his shoulder, smiled, and said, "Good morning!" Without making eye contact, he placed the palm of his hand inches from my face and said, "I can't talk to you, haven't had my coffee yet." His voice was stern and short. I took a step back, giving him a little extra space. One of my favorite things to do is *watch people* and study human behavior. It is fascinating and can actually be quite predictable. I put on my sensory acuity hat, reminding myself to be fully aware and observe.

The man ordered his complex concoction—a "large, triple soy latte, with a shot of sugar-free vanilla, hold the foam, extrahot." He then stomped over to the other counter to await his specialty drink and immediately resumed his original posture—arms crossed tight, foot tapping, hunched over. I ordered my beverage and sat down, observing him from the corner of my eye.

When his coffee was ready, the man grabbed it, inhaled a long whiff, took a sip, and instantly his whole demeanor changed. His shoulders relaxed, his chest puffed out, and a smile beamed across his face. He looked up, breathed deeply, and with a bounce in his step, pointed at me and said, "Now *you* have a nice day!" Then, I noticed the big, black letters: DECAF. I laughed. "Magic DECAF, huh?" He turned the cup to read the barista's notes, saw those inky letters of decaf doom, and growled, "Damn! They got my order wrong!" He hunched over, stormed to the counter, and began tapping his foot once more.

This man was allowing his emotional state to be influenced by a cup of coffee, but his mood wasn't really about coffee. When a person reacts disproportionately to circumstance, the experience is like being swept away by a cyclone, thrown around by winds and currents. Awareness is being in the eye of the storm. When you are centered and on purpose, nothing outside you has power over you. Instead you ride it like a wave. You choose how to perceive and give empowering meaning to your experiences.

The man in the café soon received his correct order and was on his way out the door. He glanced my way, and we smiled at each another. I introduced myself and invited him to an online teleseminar I was teaching that week on self-mastery. "Thanks," he responded. "I need all the help I can get!"

Living in Supreme Influence means you are available to the magic of the moment. One instant can change someone's life. When I extended an invitation to the man at the café, a door of opportunity opened. You have the power to give this gift to yourself and others. And when someone opens a door of opportunity for you, be grateful for the grace.

I continued observing café life and noticed how the barista masterfully guessed a number of guests' orders before they arrived at the register. She would smile, speak their order, and wait for confirmation. When the shop cleared, I walked over to her and asked, "How many people who come in here order the same drink every time?" She said, "Oh, more than eighty percent. Actually the few times where someone changes their order it throws me off—it's rare." *Fascinating,* I thought, as I looked up at the menu, which displayed myriad options of teas, herbal tonics, fresh juices, wheatgrass, specialty coffees, smoothies, nut milks, lemonades, and other blends.

Every moment contains a seed of enormous potential. But if someone chooses today as he did yesterday, without awareness, he can re-create the past and project it into the present. Of course it's okay to choose the same thing. The question is, *Are we choosing from a space of unconscious habit, or are we choosing consciously in alignment with our purpose?* When we choose with awareness we are empowered.

BECOME CONSCIOUS TO UNCONSCIOUSNESS

We've all inherited traditions, habits, and beliefs from our upbringing and societies. To evolve, it is essential to honor ancient traditions, preserving those offering life-affirming value in the now while transforming those that do not elevate our well-being. Do the rituals of our ancestors belong in today's world or to a time or consciousness of the past? Ask yourself, is this affirmation the *wisest choice*? Does it reveal doors of opportunity? Does it offer love and compassion? Does it reflect what I value and what I stand for?

Here's a parable:

Once a little girl was learning to make pot roast, a family tradition. She carefully observed her mother and learned the ritual, noticing each time her mother made pot roast, she would cut the ends off. The girl asked, "Mom, why do you always cut the ends off the pot roast before you bake it?" The mom said, "I don't know, honey. I've just always done it that way. It's the way my mom always did it. Ask Grandma." So the girl asked her grandma, "Grandma, why do you always cut the ends off the pot roast before you bake it?" Grandma said, "I'm not sure. I've always done it that way. It's the way my mom always did it. Ask Great-Grandma." So the little girl went to her great-grandma and asked, "Great-Grandma, why do you always cut the ends off the pot roast before you bake it?" Great-Grandma said, "Well, when I was growing up, we didn't have a pan big enough, and the oven was small, so we cut the ends off to make it fit."

The little girl in this parable was living in Supreme Influence—she was *curious* and would not blindly accept the status quo. She wanted to be aware; she wanted to understand.

To discern the wisest choice, first be aware that you have choice. Be aware of what you put in your body. Observe your feelings and emotional responses. What thoughts do you allow to permeate your being? Notice the words you speak and the energy you emanate. Pay attention to what is going on within you and around you during your waking and dreaming hours.

You can experience a moment of satori, which means *instant awakening*, or your awareness can unfold in stages, as reflected in the following:

Suppose an old reactive behavior comes up, such as complaining or worrying. Perhaps you may complain and only realize you're acting that way after the fact. As you continue directing your focus toward what you want, practicing conscious and deliberate awareness, you will soon pause before complaining. This is an evolutionary step. You may still complain, because the temptation is hard to resist. But acknowledging the temptation signals that you are aware. You recognize that choice is before you and that the possibility of not making the wisest choice exists. Your awareness empowers you. Soon you catch yourself before you complain, and you choose not to speak those words. The difference is now you possess discipline and strength, although the experience may still make you slightly uncomfortable. Soon you won't complain; you are neutral. Ultimately you witness the moment and move on. You are not defined or bound by material things. You understand impermanence, life, and love. You are free! You realize that *you are the door of opportunity.*

The Lotus Sutra, one of the most influential teachings in Buddhism, reveals that you are the Buddha; the Awakened One resides within each of us. The only difference between a Buddha and the average person is the degree of awareness. A regular Joe thinks he is stuck in circumstance—blaming, worrying, trying to be right or making others wrong. The Buddha is aware that who he or she is, is beyond circumstance.

Therefore, evoke your Supreme self and listen to your intuitive guidance. You can learn from others, and it is wise to do so. However, it is unwise to defer your choices to another or allow others to tell you how to think or be. Your authentic power resides in the still voice within the sanctum of your own heart.

FAITH AND GRATITUDE MANIFEST
SUPREME RESULTS

Here is a story about trusting your intuition, and having the courage to say yes to opportunity.

One Tuesday I received a call from my friend Bill, who asked, "What are you doing this weekend?"

"I'll be in my creative cocoon doing some writing," I responded. "Perhaps I'll go for a walk on the beach. Why, what's up?"

He explained he had an opportunity for me to be the keynote speaker at a company's annual convention that coming Saturday afternoon. The scheduled speaker had canceled at the last minute. "Give me the details," I said.

Bill told me about the company, explained the event was in Dallas, and said I would be speaking for sixty minutes to several hundred people. He said, "They will fly you and your assistant out, pay all expenses, but they only have a $5,000 budget for the speaker's fee." Their budget was significantly less than my usual fee, but I listened. "It's a wonderful audience," he said. "You'll love them and they'll love you. I highly recommend you do it." I was silent as he continued. "You can sell whatever you want onstage. Just pay me ten percent of your sales for putting the deal together."

I asked him to hold for a moment. I sat still, closed my eyes, and did a quick visualization exercise in my mind to discern if this deal was in alignment with my purpose. "Okay," I said, "I'll do it."

Bill asked me what I was going to sell. "My one-day Laws of Supreme Influence seminar," I responded.

"No," he said, "you have to sell a product, like a multimedia set, in the $200 to $300 price range." I explained multimedia wasn't my business. I was in the *transformational course* business. He said, "Niurka, if you don't have a product to sell, just create one."

"If I were to create a product, there's no way it'll be ready by Saturday!" I said.

"Hmm . . ." he persisted. "Sounds like a limiting belief. That's not the Niurka I know."

"Listen up," I said. "There is no way I'm going to sell something unless I feel phenomenal about it."

"Just create a flyer and a prototype," he said. "Let them know it's fresh off the press and you'll deliver it in thirty days. I've seen you do harder things in less time. You can make it happen. You're a rock star."

I told him I would call back within the hour.

I sat in my office in contemplation, then meditation, invoking Supreme wisdom. *Is this the highest choice? Maybe the Universe is bringing me this opportunity for a reason.* Part of me thought it was crazy, but the deeper part of me said, *do it.* I took a deep breath and declared . . .

I am grateful I sold two-hundred-plus units of my new multimedia set by this Saturday.

I am blessed I delivered this transformational product within thirty days, or sooner.

I am thankful it materialized instantly and properly now.
So it is.

I called my operations manager into the office and explained our goal—my transformational teachings in a multimedia set with videos, audios, and a workbook that would be valued at $250. We bounced ideas and outlined the timeline. Then he asked, "What's the title?"

I closed my eyes and inhaled a deep breath. The words *Faith & Gratitude* flashed in my mind like an aurora. "Faith and Gratitude," I declared, "because it will take both of these intelligences to pull this off!"

Step into the unknown, with faith,
and you will be given firm ground to walk on,
or wings to fly.

—INSPIRED BY EDWARD TELLER

I sighed, remembering the roles faith and gratitude played in shaping my existence. I recalled times in my past when fear had overwhelmed me. Yet I was able to navigate through it, telling myself courage isn't the absence of fear but the willingness to proceed in the face of it. I remembered Shirley Temple on Wall Street, declaring certainty in the midst of uncertainty; and countless other reaffirming references—*When put into situations demanding superhuman strength, I prevail.* The greatest gifts were not the victory and splendor of accomplishments; rather, it was who I was becoming in the process—the incarnation of my Supreme self.

I flew to Dallas, arrived on Friday, and was greeted at the airport by my driver, a man in cowboy boots, a ten-gallon hat, and a silver horseshoe–buckled belt holding up his dark blue

Levi jeans. "Howdy, Ms. Niurka. Such a pleasure to make your acquaintance. We're all very excited to hear you speak tomorrow," he said.

I smiled and replied, "Thank you, I'm delighted to be here."

The next day I arrived at the conference prepared, with my homemade prototype in hand, which looked good . . . at a distance.

Backstage, I silently spoke an affirmative prayer:

> *With love and deep reverence, I invoke for a divine blessing, knowing that the Creative Powers of the Universe are here, flowing in, as, and through me, and in, as, and through my beloveds in this room. In this space of unity, I know that every word I speak flows directly from the heart and mind of the Highest. I know the hearts and minds of the people are open and that this teaching inspires each one present to choose wisely for the accomplishment of the Great Work. I know it is done. I allow it to be. So it is. Amen.*

The owner of the company introduced me, and I entered the stage smiling. I taught how the quality of our lives is directly proportionate to the mental and emotional *states* we frequent. I illuminated how our state of mind determines what we create and attract in a universe of infinite possibility. I invoked the powers of faith and gratitude, guiding a vision of how life will unfold as we each observe reality through these potent frames. I said, "With faith, even in the midst of uncertainty, you feel certain." Faith relinquishes doubt. Then I spoke of gratitude, enlightening how this frequency presupposes abundance and thus attracts abundance to match.

I successfully delivered my sixty-minute presentation. At the end, I offered my soon-to-be-fresh-off-the-press *Faith & Gratitude: Multimedia Set* and sold over $60,000 of a product not yet created. I left Texas that evening in awe.

From the depths of my heart, to those who took action that day and purchased the original edition of *Faith & Gratitude,* THANK YOU. *Namaste. The secret's out!*

Returning home, my team and I worked day and night for weeks to ensure the product we delivered would be outstanding. A significant learning was reinforced that day: *One doesn't have to have all the ducks in a row to begin.*

When you have the courage to approach the
wall of your fear, it turns into a doorway.
Come through this door.
I AM waiting for you on the other side.

—I AM THE DOOR, PAUL FERRINI

10

CONSCIOUS CREATION

Anything you envision and believe, you can create. You are the genius mastermind behind the curtain who is responsible for every scene acted out on the stage called *your life*. As you venture forth on your journey, you are continually writing the script, casting the characters, directing the action, rearranging the set, and playing the parts. You have starred as the protagonist and the villain, the lover and the beloved. You've embodied numerous archetypes. At times you played your role so well, you forgot you were acting, finding yourself enthralled or trapped in a particular drama. But the fact you are reading this book indicates something has changed. You can step out of old paradigms and observe yourself without attachment. You have the amazing opportunity to sculpt your epic life—your reality—and inspire others along the way. This chapter reveals how your thoughts and powers of observation determine your creations.

> *All the world's a stage,*
> *And all the men and women merely players:*
> *They have their exits and their entrances;*
> *And one man in his time plays many parts.*
>
> —WILLIAM SHAKESPEARE

Now is the time for you to fully own the power you do indeed have to create your reality on purpose. You are a creator! Through your attention and intention, you attract, form, and give meaning to your life. The more you own your power to create, the more superhuman you become. Anything is possible. The only limits are the ones you acknowledge.

Let's explore what science says about how your observation of reality actually influences what shows up.

THE OBSERVER EFFECT: THE MOST BEAUTIFUL EXPERIMENT EVER

Science without religion is lame,
religion without science is blind.

—ALBERT EINSTEIN

Matter and energy are two expressions of the same essence, much like two sides of a coin. Matter released becomes energy; energy crystallized becomes matter. Matter continuously flows between energetic and material states as waves and particles. As H_2O transitions from solid ice to liquid water to gaseous steam, the essential molecules—or building blocks—remain the same, even as their physical expressions change. Similarly, the waves and particles energizing this world are in a constant state of flux.

In the past it was believed that energy and matter had properties of either a wave or a particle, but not both. This suggested a more static reality. It came as a great shock to scientists to learn that the same laws that apply to large objects do not apply to very tiny ones. Sir Isaac Newton's laws of physics do not apply at the subatomic level, where matter exhibits properties of waves *and* particles. In one moment, matter or energy could be moving around in a nebulous, free-flowing waveform pattern with no definitive fixed location in space. In the next, they can crystallize into a particle whose location could be specifically pinpointed. This discovery led to the realization that reality exists as a probability of becoming, rather than an absolute and immutable fact! A certain result may be more likely to manifest, but waves of possibility only crystallize into definitive substances when an observer is witnessing to measure the result.

Physicist Thomas Young conducted an experiment known as "the double slit" that proved matter exhibits properties of both waves *and* particles. This experiment was heralded as "the most beautiful experiment ever" and resulted in a discovery later dubbed the "observer effect."

The observer effect confirms scientifically that the process of observation actually influences what shows up. This affirms that your attention and intention have materializing power!

The physical world, including our bodies,
is a response of the observer.
We create our bodies as we create
the experience of our world.
—DEEPAK CHOPRA

Scientists first became aware of the phenomenon of energy taking form as waves and particles by studying light. Scientists would fire a beam of light—one photon at a time—through two slits in a piece of paper and observe the pattern on the photographic plate behind it. The patterns on the photographic plate surprised the scientists.

When a single particle was fired through a double slit, it arrived on the other side as a single particle, as expected. But when several single particles were fired one at a time, in succession through the double slit, an interference pattern appeared, which indicated that light exhibits properties of a wave. The light was launched as a particle; it simultaneously passed through both slits, behaving like a wave of potential energy, then collapsed onto the photographic plate as a particle again.

This greatly confused scientists. So they decided to measure what happened at the precise moment the light passed through the double slit. Was it a wave or a particle? They discovered that when observed, the particle passes through the double slit as a particle, creating the expected pattern of two double lines on the photographic plate.

To clarify: When observed, light exhibits properties of a particle. But when not observed, it appears as a wave of potential. It doesn't seem to have a fixed location in space until it is observed.

Ultimately, the observer determines what form will appear. If the scientist looks for a particle using a particle detector, then a particle is found. However, if the scientist looks for a wave with a wave detector, a wave is found. A quantum entity like light has a dual potential nature, but its actual nature manifests as what is observed. This is the observer effect. It has massive implications for how you create your experience of reality. No wonder the observer effect is referred to as "the most beautiful experiment ever."

*If quantum mechanics hasn't profoundly shocked
you, you haven't understood it yet.*
—NIELS BOHR, PHYSICIST

Reality is not static; it is in a continual dance of transformation, which means nothing in your life—however real or fixed it may appear—is permanent. All is in constant flow responding to the power of your thought and observation. This means that you can influence the outcome of events by influencing yourself to imagine and focus steadily on what you want.

When I study science, I don't only observe facts. By delving deeper than the readily observable data, I locate applicable patterns for my own life. What wisdom can I gain from the double-slit experiment? Again and again I have learned to live in the flow of life, open and alert to endless possibilities, while consciously willing my intent into existence. Surrendering my grip and letting go of preconceived ideas, I seek to discover all that can be found to support conscious evolution.

Through my observation and declaration, I have materialized desires out of chaos. My manifestations are the Universe echoing back the reflection of my consciousness—my dominant thoughts, internal representations, and corresponding vibrations.

THOUGHT FORMS MATERIALIZE AS MATTER

In the not-too-distant past, we had grown accustomed to looking at the world and seeing physical matter, thinking the physical was more real than other, more subtle frequencies, like thought. However, everything in the material world emanated from the realm of thought. An object began as an idea in the imagination, then crystallized into form through visualization and vocalization. Tables, chairs, roads, cars, houses, clothes, tangible items—all began as thought in someone's mind before being summoned into existence.

Thought may be a subtler frequency than matter, but thoughts have magnetic force, especially the thoughts you continually think about. Thoughts fueled by emotion, focus, and repetition become thought forms. Thought forms attract to you what you think about most often and with passion. A thought form is a vivid internal representation having definitive substance. These thought forms are projected onto the canvas of life and shape our world. This is the basis of *perception is projection*; this is how you create reality.

Songs, poems, and stories do not have form as tangible matter you can see or touch, but they are very real in our experience and in the feelings and emotions they evoke. A painter sees a painting before it is painted. Before pigment touches canvas, the painting exists in the mind's eye—it is a thought form. Remember when I quoted Vincent van Gogh: "I dream my paintings and then paint my dreams." Though it doesn't yet have physical form, the thought form exists in a dimension of consciousness.

An idea can also take shape as thought forms. It can be fueled by multiple and continual thoughts about it. Thought forms can outlive our bodies. Corporations exist as thought forms. They actually have legal rights as people do, even though corporations do not necessarily exist as something you can see or touch. They are bodyless entities, but no less real in our experience. Ideas—like capitalism, democracy, and civil rights—are thought forms. We have created concepts like these, and they have been structured and ordained through our collective attention and conversation. These concepts affect our lives—how we view, sustain, and experience reality in the midst of infinite possibility. It's important to remember *it's the mind of man that created them.* Since we conceived them, we can transform, elevate, and align them with our vision.

THE GIFT THAT MULTIPLIES

Here's a story about how thought forms materialize as matter.

Years ago I experienced a series of months where challenges appeared to beam at me from myriad directions—broken relationship, broken leg, broken investments. While navigating the chaos, I intuited it was time to cocoon and restore my equilibrium before determining how to proceed. I completed my commitments and embarked to Bali on a creative sabbatical and journey of healing.

Bali is a mystical place, grounded in tradition, ritual, and prayer, and the land was calling me into deep contemplation and rejuvenation. On my first morning, I woke before sunrise and walked along the beach, whispering a mantra from my core and appreciating Gaia's (Mother Earth's) gifts. As the first golden rays of sunlight reached over the horizon, I smiled and raised my hands in adoration to the sun—*Hail unto thee who art Ra in thy rising!* This is one of my prayer rituals that attunes me to the rhythms of nature and reminds me of the interconnectivity of all life.

In Egyptian cosmology, Ra is the god of the sun, who is central to a number of creation myths. In my salutation I give thanks to the energy and consciousness of the sun, the unique essence that warms us and gives life on this planet. You may have seen this symbol. It's called the Eye of Ra.

After a few weeks of meditation along a secluded coast in Bali, I intuited it was time to explore more of this magical island. I found my way to a remote temple with springwater flowing through nine stone pipes inwardly carved with ancient Sanskrit writing. Above each spout was a statue of a deity. Bali honors many different gods as aspects of One Supreme Source, who has innumerable emanations. Just as you are one being with many names—Susan, Ms. Smith, Mom, Lover, Goddess, Suzy, and so on—each name evokes a unique aspect of the infinite you. Each deity represents a unique aspect of the One Consciousness that is alive within each of us—*as in the microcosm, so in the macrocosm.* One statue represents wisdom; another, understanding; the other, beauty. Each deity presents a mudra, a symbolic hand gesture that evokes a mental state, advances concentration, and offers blessings. Several deities also hold a magic weapon particular to their form of consciousness. In Balinese spirituality, "weapons" can be sacred instruments that aid in concentration and invoke the forces of nature. In this context, weapons are wielded for a divine purpose. Another deity in the temple holds the *bajra*, a bell that, according to the *manku* (high priest), corresponds to the direction east, where Ra rises, and the power of the Logos, which he honored as *Om*.

I left the temple stimulated and serendipitously found my way to Ubud, the cultural center and a bustling town. Balinese women in traditional sarongs stand chatting in storefronts, selling beautifully handcrafted works of art. Everywhere you go, incense burns as prayer offerings. I strolled down the main street, Monkey Forest Road, with its canopy of trees and wild monkeys roaming the streets, dodging the mopeds zipping by. Inspired by my temple adventure and the handmade treasures I saw on my path, I got a brilliant idea. *I will create a talisman, a ring crafted from my consciousness that I will carry from temple to temple! I will bless, charge, and consecrate it to the service of the Supreme.* This ring would be an anchor, imbued with the frequencies of my devoted meditation. I knew I had to attract a special craftsman—not just any jeweler, but one who had purity of spirit and esoteric understanding. One who could grasp the profundity of my intent.

As I walked, I began cultivating an internal representation of the talisman. In my mind's eye, I could see gold, silver, onyx, diamonds, and rubies, beautifully arranged with carvings of a Sanskrit mantra on one side. The tetragrammaton—יהוה, four Hebrew letters corresponding to YHWH, the holiest unspoken name of God—raised upon the uppermost layer. And my own sigil on the base.

A sigil is a consecrated symbol created for a specific purpose. Here is my company's sigil. It symbolizes the Creative Powers of the Universe (the sacred masculine and divine feminine) coming together to birth all of creation.

The ring began crystallizing in my mind. I looked down at my left hand and could see it as done. In that instant, I knew with certainty I would attract my *anam cara* (my soul friend), the one with a pure heart who would consciously build this treasure.

With high concentration, I projected the picture in my mind onto the canvas of life and summoned the artist I could entrust with this piece. I barely finished uttering my affirmative prayer when I looked up and an enormous, beautiful sign appeared above a small jewelry shop as if created for that moment. It read: SERAPHIM. Instantly, I knew I had been guided. The Seraphim are an order of angels; this was no coincidence. I walked into the Seraphim shop and was greeted by a beautiful young Balinese girl in traditional garb and black-rimmed glasses. Immediately she asked if I wished to meet the owner. Yes, I said, and she stepped out.

I looked around the shop in awe at the stunning pieces of jewelry. Each was one of a kind, adorned with a handwritten note describing it. Behind the wide desk at the end of the shop were several photos of a jolly Balinese man shaking hands with celebrities and dignitaries from around the world. In one photo was Jimmy Carter; in another, Demi Moore.

Suddenly, from behind the back curtain, out sprang the man in the photos—a portly man with a huge grin and white sarong. His presence was grand, and his cheer bounced off the walls and ceilings. I felt an instant connection, intuiting *he is the one*. I remained alert and unattached. We simultaneously folded our hands before our hearts in prayer position, head slightly bowed, while speaking the traditional Balinese greeting, *Om swastiastu* (the equivalent of *Namaste*, meaning "The divine in me sees, recognizes, and honors the divine in you"). Then, in a royal tone, he declared, "I am Ra!"

"Of course you are," I said, while basking in the glory of the magic moment as I remembered my daily sun adoration, adding, "I am Niurka." We held our gaze for a timeless moment in silent recognition. Our meeting was destiny.

I explained my purpose, who I am, and how his shop materialized the moment I clearly saw what I wanted in my mind and declared it so. I disclosed details of my intent while keenly observing how he received my communication. He lit up, became very intense, grabbed both my hands, stared directly into my eyes, and firmly asked, "Are you going to help the people?"

"Yes," I solidly said. "I will and I do."

We were tuned in; we were not just communicating with words but through energetic intent. Ra lowered his voice and said, "This is destiny. Because you help the people, I will make you the most powerful sacred weapon in Bali!" Ra took out a piece of paper and proceeded to draw me a map. Not just any map. This was a map constructed with layers of understanding of astrology, cosmology, ritual, and Balinese history, lore, mythology, and spirituality.

He explained that I was to purify my body: to venture to various temples across Bali and meet with *mankus* (high priests) and *balians* (shamanic healers), bringing special offerings, reciting secret mantras, and securing holy water and other select items kept in the most holy, hidden center of the temples and released only under hallowed circumstances. I was to climb mountains and pray in temples at the stroke of midnight, invoking the Creative Powers on the full and dark moon before *mukimit* (sleeping in the temple till sunrise). This was a two-month treasure hunt in a mysterious land, divinely orchestrated to ensure optimum energetic power. One part of me thought, *This is crazy.* Another part countered, *This is an adventure of a lifetime.* I looked at him and said, "You must come with me."

He replied: "You talk to my wife; if she says yes, I will go."

Ra then took out another piece of paper, and together we designed the ring. I was so enwrapped in the moment that I forgot my assistant was arriving at the airport. I often brought her on my adventures. Instantly, I realized I couldn't create a talisman of this caliber for me and not have something designed for her. I paused and went within, listening to my own inner wisdom. What shall I design for her? The answer immediately came. I looked at Ra and said, "We must craft another piece—an amulet." He instantly connected with my thoughts and began sketching. He drew a circle and placed my sigil in the center, then drew eight concentric circles representing the protective forces of the universe from all directions. While he drew, images of my dearest friends back home emerged in my consciousness. The voice in my head said: *Create 111 pieces.* Instantly, I got a vivid internal representation of myself giving this gift to the most cherished people in my life and feeling joy in doing so. Ideas were flowing. I said to Ra, "We will number each amulet, so each is one of a kind. I will place the name of each bearer in a holy book, which will sit upon my altar."

Initially I intended to create one talisman for me, then one amulet for my assistant. Through my desire to give and share, my one magical piece multiplied like Jesus's loaves and fishes. Once I returned home, I gave my beloveds their gifts. Soon, a buzz evolved about the amulets, and people began inquiring on

how to acquire one. My creative sabbatical and journey of healing advanced into a profitable sacred adventure rich with gifts
for those whom I love.

Now all of us wearing this sacred piece are part of one
tribe who recognize one another's magnificence and hold one
another in our prayers and meditations. We know we don't *need*
any object to call forth our creative powers, for those are inherent. As long as we choose to wear something on our body temple, we agree it makes sense to ensure it is crafted consciously.
And so it is.

In Bali I imagined and declared my intent. Then I paid
attention, and the signs pointed the way. Guided by my intuition, I was clear about what I wanted, I was receptive, and the
next step was revealed.

When we are in the flow of life, we create with ease and
grace. The people, places, and things that can support us
miraculously appear. Synchronicity abounds. When we focus

on giving, the Universe delights us with gifts and blessings. It's in the giving that we receive. This is creative consciousness. This is living in Supreme Influence.

Nothing real can be increased,
except by sharing.

—A COURSE IN MIRACLES

SECTION III

EMPOWER

11

ABRACADABRA

Words and magic were in the beginning one and
the same thing, and even today words retain much
of their magical power. By words one of us can
give another the greatest happiness or bring about
utter despair; by words the teacher imparts his
knowledge to the student; by words the orator
sweeps his audience with him and determines
its judgments and decisions. Words call forth
emotions and are universally the means by which
we influence our fellow-creatures.

—SIGMUND FREUD

As a child I was fascinated with magic. When David Copper-
field, the great illusionist, caused the Statue of Liberty to disappear, I was enthralled. In that moment I knew there was more
to life than what meets the eye, and I wanted to discover it;
I wanted to unveil the Great Mystery. So I started sincerely
searching, and as I did, life delighted me with clues.

One day, while at a park, I met a magician who asked if I'd
like to see his act. "Yes," I enthusiastically replied.

"Stand back," he said. "I shall now pull a rabbit out of this
empty top hat—*Abracadabra!*" And the seemingly "impossible"
was accomplished.

Over the years I came to learn that the word *abracadabra* closely translates to "I create as I speak," in Aramaic. *Abra* means "to create" and *cadabra* means "as I say."

The magician's game pointed to a deeper esoteric truth—*our language has magical power*. Look at the etymology of the word *magic* and you will learn that the meaning has changed over the last few centuries. In the late 1400s, *magic* meant the "art of influencing events and producing marvels using hidden natural forces." Our thoughts and imagination are examples of these "hidden natural forces" that we use to create. Wielding them consciously is Supreme Influence.

One day I woke up and realized what magic *really* is, and that I am the magician. Now, I show others how they too are the magician.

What do I mean by "magician"?

I am not referring to a stage magician who inspires awe by performing feats that defy human logic. I am referring to a magi, one who is skilled in invoking and directing the forces of nature to accomplish a specific aim.

The terms *magic* and *magician* have acquired a limited and at times even negative connotation. Magic has been associated with deception, and magicians relegated to entertainers. To grasp the true essence and power of magic requires deeper esoteric understanding.

The term *magus* has been used since before the fourth century BC and has had multiple meanings. In the Gospel of Matthew 2:1–12, the "wise men from the East" are Magi who intuit that a new King was to be born. These sagacious men traveled far to honor and bestow sacred gifts upon the infant Jesus. How did these wise men know this momentous event was about to unfold? According to the Bible, the wise men saw a luminous bright star rise from the east. They were attuned to the celestial energetic patterns of the constellations.

Genuine magicians have integrated knowledge of their own divine nature and the workings of energy. Honoring their oneness with the Supreme, they wield their thoughts and words to consciously create. They are vast and obscure— human and immortal. They walk among us yet live in eternity. They are masters of high concentration. Disciplined and with stable mind, they speak with the authority and precision of the Logos—and the universe responds to the power of their command. Hence, their word is made flesh. *Abracadabra!*

I CREATE AS I SPEAK

I: "I" is the authority to call forth and attract what you envision. When you say "I," you own your "I am" presence, which is the union of Supreme and human consciousness activated through your awareness, intention, and vocalization.

CREATE: "Create" is your focused thought moving into conscious action. It is your ability to bring forth order from chaos. Although the word *chaos* has connotations of disorder and confusion, it originally meant "formless or void." According to Greek mythology and the big bang theorists, our entire universe was birthed from "chaos," the great wide-open void of infinite potentialities. Even the story of Genesis says, "In the beginning when God created the heavens and the earth, the earth was a *formless void.*"

Therefore, "chaos" is *really* that which precedes creation. It is the potential from which you consciously create your imaginings.

When you say "I create," you own your power to summon order from chaos, in any situation.

SPEAK: "Speak" is your influence. It is how you consciously wield your thoughts, words, and deeds to produce a desired result. When you "speak" you translate the idea in your mind (your creation) into tangible reality. "Speak" embodies the fullness of your communication—what you declare (both aloud and to yourself), your body language, your expressions, your written word, your actions, and your energetic intent. You speak through words, a look, a gesture, a touch, a breath, a posture, a gift, a sound, a facial expression, a mood, a note, and more.

Say out loud "I CREATE AS I SPEAK," and feel the power you indeed have to sculpt your reality.

The Living One . . . created the
universe . . . with . . . words.
—SEPHIR YETZIRAH (BOOK OF CREATION)

BLESSINGS AND CURSES

It is said that with great power comes great responsibility. And so it is.

One Saturday afternoon I was outside enjoying my garden, when my neighbor pulled in to her driveway. She saw me outside and came over to say hello. She looked disturbed. We began chatting, and she told me that a few days earlier someone had stolen her scissors. She was a beautician and had just purchased these special scissors. I asked her if she was sure she hadn't misplaced them. In a boiling tone she barked, "No! I know exactly where I left them in my drawer, and I know for a fact who stole them." I asked her how she knew. She said, "Because right after I realized they were stolen I shouted, 'Whoever stole my scissors, I hope their fingers fall off!' Then," she said, "a few days later I heard that the delivery man who worked for one of my vendors was helping a friend lay a new roof and molten tar spilled on his hands."

Regardless of what really happened, in the Middle Ages, her words would have been considered a curse. A curse is an expressed wish for adversity or misfortune to befall someone. It is a form of black magic, which most commonly occurs unconsciously when a person declares something in an intensely charged emotional state, such as anger. Speaking a curse has karmic repercussions because it's in the giving that we receive. Curses result from ignorance. In that moment, the person forgets her authentic Self and loses control. The divine spark has been smothered by negative thought forms, which are disempowering thoughts that have been fueled with emotion and repetition.

Your words have heightened materializing power when they're backed by strong emotion, whether empowering or disempowering. If you feel a surge of energy, you can harness and transmute it. Through intentional transference of energy, you spark evolution and inspire those around you.

First learn the meaning of what you say,
and then speak.

—EPICTETUS

You can be light unto darkness. If you walk into a dark room and want light, what do you do? Flip on the switch. You are light that can rekindle another's flame. The first step: consciously observe *what is*, in a state of total presence without judgment. I call this *holding sacred space*. See beyond shadows into the Supreme essence animating life, each being's inner divine flame. Through your pure reflection and heightened vibration, you cause those who've forgotten to remember. You can perform miracles of transforming darkness into light—you have the power to illuminate the universe! You are a star.

If there is light in the soul, there will be beauty
in the person. If there is beauty in the person,
there will be harmony in the house. If there is
harmony in the house, there will be order in
the nation. If there is order in the nation,
there will be peace in the world.

—CHINESE PROVERB

A treasured gift you can offer is your blessing. A blessing is a prayer consciously and lovingly spoken from the depth of your heart, with Supreme authority, bestowing grace on the recipient. Traditionally a man will ask another man's blessing for his daughter's hand in marriage. This ritual, leading up to a rite of passage, honors families and creates a harmonious atmosphere for us all to flourish. These are keys to building conscious community. Bless your family; bless your children; bless the world's children. Bless our beloved Gaia, Mother Earth; bless Ra, the majestic sun, our solar system, and Milky Way galaxy. Bless your heart. As I was writing about blessings, my mom called and bestowed a blessing upon me. I thankfully receive and bless her. Amazing! We do speak into existence!

Here's a blessing for your beloved:

May your day be radiant and resplendent, filled with joy, peace, and love. May you be bold, authentic, and true to your heart. May you breathe in ease and grace, knowing you are a perfect expression of divinity in human form. May you know your own magnificence and allow your light to shine for all to see! May your health, wealth, and relationships be blessed. May you live your purpose and manifest your vision. And so it is.

Your blessings don't have to be long. They can be short and powerful. It's up to you. Just speak from the infinite depths of your beautiful heart and enjoy giving the gift.

You can also bless things. For example, I find great pleasure and power in blessing food. I speak to my food with gratitude, honoring it for offering itself unto me. I see my blessing penetrate through the food chain back to the hands that cultivated it and back to the earth and sun. This ritual affirms my sacred union with existence. It purifies my mind, activates my cells, and prepares my body temple to receive nutrients.

When someone offers you a blessing, be receptive. It's the Universe giving you a gift.

12

THE FORMULA FOR CONSCIOUS CREATION

Everything in your life—what you love and what you'd love to change—has been summoned into your experience by you. It reflects the consciousness and perspective you've held up until now. Your reality is an echo of what you've been thinking, perceiving, feeling, and doing. This is good news! It means that you can change your reality simply by changing your mind.

In this chapter, I will share with you a formula for conscious creation. I've applied it countless times and rapidly manifested miracles in my own life. I've also taught it in my Magickal Materialization course, which I created by applying these exact principles. And my students have applied this formula to produce consistent outstanding results in their lives.

PREREQUISITE TO CONSCIOUS CREATION

Before we explore the formula, there is one prerequisite to master your powers of conscious creation:

Take responsibility for everything (past/present/future)
unfolding in your life, without attachment.

What do I mean? I mean you take ownership (no ifs, ands, or buts) for every result in your life, realizing that at some level you attracted or created it. This isn't about blame. It's about freedom. If you created it, you can transform it. You are aware that in any given moment you are either "at cause" in your life or "in effect." NLP explains this as an equation.

CAUSE>EFFECT:
RESULTS VS. REASONS

Living "at cause" means you accept responsibility for your entire experience of reality. You take personal accountability, without judgment, for everything that manifests in your life. You own your results—all of them, the light, the shadow, and everything in between. Owning results, desired or not, liberates you to change course on demand.

Conversely, anytime you give an excuse, blame, or complain, you are "in effect." Being "in effect" means you've temporarily given up your power. When someone is "in effect," his communication reflects it. He worries, criticizes, reacts disproportionately to circumstance, or checks out. Being "in effect" is playing the role of persecutor or victim. It's shifting the focus to the environment rather than one's own mind or inner power to create change.

You are the grand architect. You are more powerful than any challenge in your life. No matter what, you can direct your focus and choose your response. You are *response-able*—able to consciously respond, in each instant, regardless of circumstance. How you respond to life paves the way for future manifestations. Even in the midst of a challenge, or a titanic miscommunication, and even if you feel a severe response is justified, you are capable of making a chivalrous choice in word and deed. While you are not responsible for the actions of another, you are able to consciously respond to everything in *your* reality. Your power to respond is your power to create. The *quality* of your response influences corresponding responses and the subsequent chain of events.

Living in Supreme Influence, you are "at cause" and *response-able*. You bring your totality to the present—fully awake, fully alive, and fully here.

Now, are you ready to integrate this potent formula for conscious creation?

THE TEN-STEP FORMULA
FOR CONSCIOUS CREATION

Here is the Supreme Influence ten-step formula for conscious creation. As you read, allow your consciousness and imagination to explore each of the steps, one at a time. Apply each one to achieve your vision.

1. Observe "what is" with courage and without attachment.
2. Choose what you intend to create or experience.
3. Check in. Ensure you are on purpose.
4. See, hear, and feel the end result accomplished in your mind's eye.
5. Model success and create a milestone.

6. Amplify the pictures, sounds, and feelings in your mind.
7. Declare what you want with authority and know it is done.
8. Act without lust for result.
9. Be ready and alert.
10. Allow life to unfold.

Let's explore these ten steps.

Observe

Look around at your circumstances. How are you being? What are you doing? What has shown up in your health, finances, relationships, business, and your overall quality of life? Pause for a moment and observe *what is*. Does the "what is" around you reflect the "what is" inside of you? Does your life mirror what you value? It might seem easier to observe *what is* when *what is* reflects what you want. However, often the very thing that challenges you is where the greatest gift resides for your evolution.

Let me not pray to be sheltered from dangers,
but to be fearless in facing them.
Let me not beg for the stilling of my pain,
but for the heart to conquer it.
—RABINDRANATH TAGORE

Many things in the world appear harsh or burdensome. Many people suffer through illness, injustice, or loss. At times it can seem easier to avoid or deny difficulty. Although it is wise to focus on what you want versus what you don't want, looking away from adversity doesn't necessarily make it disappear. Albert Einstein said, "Knowledge of what is does not open the door directly to what should be." Observe and see through *what is* into *what could be*. Do not run, hide, pretend, or cover anything up. *You are a creator.* I am not exaggerating. You can activate your will to transform circumstance. Whatever appears as a problem, courageously face it, and you will have the power to alchemize it. Summon a grounded, neutral, and resourceful mental/emotional state. If you experience destructive emotions like anger or fear in the presence of *what is*, you can welcome these frequencies and transmute them into fuel. This is what Gandhi did: he observed injustice (the *what is*) without looking away and transmuted his anger into the evolutionary impulse that led India to independence and inspired global nonviolent movements for civil rights and freedom. In Buddhism this process is known as "hendoku-iyaku," or turning poison into medicine.

I have learned through bitter experience the one supreme lesson to conserve my anger, and as heat conserved is transmuted into energy, even so our anger controlled can be transmuted into a power that can move the world.

—MAHATMA GANDHI

If you feel caught up in the drama of *what is*, feeling uncontrolled emotions, then pause, center your physiology, inhale a deep breath, and as you exhale . . . step outside yourself for a moment.

Pretend you are in a movie theater, sitting all the way in the back eating popcorn and watching the *you* on the screen go through the particular drama. You can even make the movie black and white, or a silent film, Charlie Chaplin style. Now ask yourself, "What can she learn? What is the highest choice?" Often the contrast of not wanting *what is* sparks a new worthwhile desire and motivation. Allow *what is* to brew in your consciousness, just enough to know what you really do want. Then . . .

Choose

Now it is time to choose what you want. What do you desire? What is your ultimate outcome? Be specific without becoming attached to how it will show up. Ask yourself, *If I could create anything, what would it be? If I could give people anything, what would I give? What do I want to experience? What would I choose if I had no fear? What would love do?*

It is imperative you make up your mind. The word *imperative* has its root in an old Latin verb meaning "to set in order." Having a clear objective gives you direction and harmonizes your life with divine order. Hopes and wishes are faint. A genuine choice guides action.

Check In

Check to ensure that what you want matches your true purpose. You will know your choice is a wise one because:

- It does not infringe upon the will of another.
- It feels good for you.
- It is a unique expression of your rare talents.

- No part of you objects to experiencing or
  materializing it.
- There are multiple ways to achieve it.
- It is self-initiated and self-maintained; in other words,
  you are not dependent on any one person or thing for its
  accomplishment.

See, Hear, and Feel

Once you have *observed* what is, you've *chosen* what you want,
and you know it's in alignment with your true purpose, you can
begin forming, coloring, and energizing a crystal-clear mental
image. How will you know when you achieve your goal? What
will you see? What will you hear and feel that will signal the
realization of your chosen aim? Think of the end result accomplished and, as you do, notice the pictures, sounds, and feelings
in your mind's eye. Feel the sensations in your body as though
it is done. Focus on experiencing the essence of your desired
result without getting caught up in having it materialize in a
particular way.

Model and Milestone

If someone can achieve a result, others can learn to achieve it.
You don't need to reinvent the wheel. You can seek out, research,
and learn from the successes of others. Who do you know that
is a model of possibility? Who is creating success in a way that
inspires you? You have role models all around you. You can find
masters in myriad ways, serendipitously: in books, on the Internet,
via friends, through social media. You could do your homework,
discover what a mentor likes, and give that person a thoughtful

gift. Reach out with a letter, a testimonial, an offering, or something that shows your appreciation. Allow your new learnings to stimulate your thoughts and blend with your gifts. Now what is the first, most important milestone *you* intend to accomplish?

Amplify

Think about what you want. As you do, carefully observe the pictures, sounds, feelings, smells, and tastes in your mind's eye. Then amplify your senses. Make the image big, bright, crisp, clear—gently turn up the volume, feel it in your bones and loins. See it, hear it, feel it, smell it, taste it, breathe it in. Make sure you are looking through your own eyes. Magnify and intensify the experience until you slip into timelessness. You are no longer bound by time and space, you are in eternity, and the Creative Powers are within you—and surrounding you. Now, with certainty and without attachment, firmly hold your attention and concentration. You are free, creating for the sheer enjoyment of expressing your godlike nature. Next, double the intensity—feel the energy spinning within you. Feel it flowing and snaking up and down your spine like a fluid figure eight. The moment will come when you sense triumph. In that instant you have crystallized your internal representation. Feel gratitude, knowing your vision is achieved.

Your vision will become clear only when you can
look into your own heart. Who looks outside,
dreams; who looks inside, awakens.

—CARL JUNG

Declare and Know

At the moment your state peaks and you feel a sense of certainty, in that instant speak your goal into existence. Vocalize that which is already done in your heart and mind. Be bold; be succinct. Speak with authority and write it down on a clean piece of paper. Use a thick red pen, and write your declaration as though it is accomplished now, like this:

> *I am grateful that* _____ *(insert a brief description of your goal as accomplished) or greater has materialized by* _____ *(date) or sooner.*
> *So it is!*

Concentrate as you speak and write. You must be single-minded in focus. Fuel your words with your energetic intent. See your internal representation projecting onto the canvas of life. Know it is done, release it into the Universe, and allow it to be.

By the Word of the Lord the heavens were made, and all their host by the breath of His mouth ... For he spoke, and it was done; he commanded, and it stood firm.

–PSALMS 33:6,9

Act

Now that you've crystallized your internal representation and spoken it into existence, it is time to take focused, inspired action. Sometimes the wisest action is inaction, or refraining from taking hasty or ignorant action. The Bhagavad Gita, a sacred Sanskrit scripture that speaks deeply to my soul, states, "One who sees inaction in action, and action in inaction, is intelligent among mankind. He has attained the goal of all actions and is free." The key is awareness and purposeful action without attachment. Relinquish lust for result. This is the Supreme way of life, because you rest in the knowing of *who you are* and *why you are here*. You are whole and complete, and creating not from a place of need but rather from the sacred space of love and devotion. Your creation is your offering unto the Supreme; it's your art—your consecrated gift to your self and humanity.

Attachment kills materializing power because it is grounded in fear and separation. Attachment presupposes absence or lack, and since you are a vibrational being, whatever vibe you emanate will boomerang back. Just like the echo in the book of Genesis—"*Be light*," *light be*. Trust the Universe and do your work. Know that when you plant tomato seeds and honor the cycles of nature, your crop is assured. Even if tomatoes are not the result, know something even better; the essence of your authentic desire is under way. Take action and trust the Creative Powers to do your bidding—at the proper time.

In the Bhagavad Gita, Krishna, revered as the manifestation of the Supreme, councils the epic hero, Arjuna, in the midst of a crisis. Krishna guides Arjuna in practicing karma yoga. *Karma* means action; *yoga* means union. Therefore, the literal translation of *karma yoga* is the path of union through action. In this ancient text, Krishna says to Arjuna, "Therefore, without being attached to the fruits of action, one should act as a matter of sacred duty, for by working without attachment one attains the Supreme."

There is freedom and authentic joy in offering attachment to the fruits of action as a *sacrifice* unto the Highest. The word *sacrifice* has been misinterpreted to mean "giving up one's self to a greater cause," or even "killing a living being to appease an angry god." These misinterpretations have linked pain and suffering to the notion of sacrifice, but these meanings are light-years away from the deeper significance of sacrifice: *to make sacred.* By sacrificing the fruits of action, you consecrate it as a holy offering unto the Supreme self. You can still relish and share in the fruit; you just don't cling to it. Therefore, work and find ecstasy in working. Honor the ebb and flow of life itself. Live in the wisdom of immortality, for only a consciousness trapped in fear would hoard that which will turn to dust. Your spirit is eternal. Supreme Influence grounds the eternal within the backdrop of time and space.

My actions are my only true belongings. I cannot escape the consequences of my actions. My actions are the ground upon which I stand.
—THICH NHAT HANH

Be Ready

Pay attention. Allow your awareness to expand into peripheral vision. Heighten your senses by observing the subtleties of how you feel and the rich details all around you. Be mindful, alert, and ready. You will begin noticing signs and signals pointing you in the direction you want to go. Being on purpose, the Universe conspires to delight you, bringing you the essence of your desires, often even more magnificent than you imagined. Be watchful and receptive. Auspicious and serendipitous encounters will spontaneously cross your path. When they do, listen to your intuition and act accordingly. Honor your feelings, and they will point the way. And most of all . . . enjoy the ride.

Allow

Now it's time to let nature take its course. It's up to you to implement the formula for Supreme creation, but it's not up to you to micromanage the details. Just as with the practice of archery, you center your being, become still, focus on a target, and launch the arrow of your genuine intent toward the bull's-eye. But the moment you release the arrow, you must let go. Release the desire to make the arrow fly the way you hope or think it should. Allow the arrow to fly unencumbered.

When you apply this ten-step formula, you will access superhuman strength to consciously create your reality. The next chapter shares stories and suggestions that reveal how.

|||||||||||||||||||||||||| **SUPREME BONUS** ||||||||||||||||||||||||||

Enriching Your Map of the World
by Heightening Your Senses

Enriching your map of the world supports you in consciously creating a life you love. One way to enrich your mental map is by heightening your senses, thus tuning into subtler energies. As you do this, you will make new distinctions and enjoy life at a deeper, richer, more fulfilling level than ever before.

We filter the sea of information through our senses, or neurological constraints. Unlike beliefs and memories (individual constraints), our physical sensory filters work with information presented in the now. Your body is in present time. Your mind may wander to thoughts of the past or future, but your body is only in the present moment.

Our physical senses allow us to interpret the frequencies surrounding us. Our sense of hearing allows us to receive intelligence about sound vibrations in our experience. Our sense of smell receives frequencies in the range of olfactory information. The same applies to our sense of touch—our kinesthetic sense—allowing us to feel heat, where we are in space, pain, balance, and acceleration. Our eyesight picks up a wide spectrum of light frequencies, and our taste absorbs a range of stimuli. Our physical senses act like receptors, picking up data and transmitting them through our nervous system and brain, communicating the information in a way that we can respond to the world around us.

Other creatures have filters they rely on more strongly. Birds and bees rely on their sense of magnetism for direction. This is as important to them as the sense of smell is to dogs. These enhanced senses and unique filters cause these animals to perceive things most humans do not.

We have finer senses not traditionally acknowledged that also play a role in what information we receive from the world around us. For example, we can tap into our intuitive senses of clairvoyance and clairsentience. We access these by amplifying our awareness and tuning in to the subtler realms, which provides more information. Not long ago, heightened sensory experiences were dismissed as "paranormal" or feared as witchcraft. History books are filled with stories of people who were burned at the stake for tapping into these senses. However, these extrasensory perceptions are natural. They are levels of awareness available to each one of us when we pierce the veils of what has ordinarily been defined as "reality."

These heightened senses develop with practice. As you develop them, you will realize a fuller spectrum of experience. You will receive clearer information and guidance from nature. You will also communicate more clearly when you are aware of more subtle realms.

How can you tune in to your subtler senses? It's simply a matter of focus and receptivity. Pay attention to the empty spaces between moments. Let's do an exercise. Go grab a big, red apple. Now, prepare to eat the apple; give the experience your undivided attention. Smell the apple before you bite into it. Allow the aroma to overwhelm you before it crosses your lips. Notice the texture through your fingertips, and the shape and weight in your hands. Observe the transitions of color, the sense of moisture inside. As the apple enters your mouth, you penetrate its flesh and let the flavor dissolve on your tongue. Listen for the crunch; hear yourself chew. Notice the wetness and texture as you masticate and the apple morphs from solid to liquid. When you swallow, feel the apple essence cascading down your throat. Slow down time. Honor the space between bites, between breaths. The more alive your senses are, the juicier and richer life becomes. It's a simple practice for presence.

This practice is not just about enjoying your meals; it's about bringing the fullness of your consciousness to life. This has benefits in every area of your existence, whether you're sitting at a business meeting and you naturally recognize distinctions that others would miss or you are playing with your child and relishing the moment. Heightening your senses is a choice, as the old adage says, to stop and smell the roses. And when you do . . . and you enjoy smelling them and looking at them . . . you will enjoy life.

13

I CREATE MY REALITY

Andrew Carnegie immigrated to America with pennies in his pocket and became a self-made multimillionaire and one of the most important philanthropists of his era. He believed the process of success had a formula anyone who understood could apply. He commissioned a man named Napoleon Hill to interview and study the most successful and wealthiest people of his time. Hill authored the highly influential books *The Law of Success* and *Think and Grow Rich,* which detailed how achievement occurs.

Hill said:

> *My search led me to study the spiritual forces with*
> *which all of us are blessed. And . . . I came*
> *upon a clue, which has enabled me to help millions*
> *of people to find their earthly destinies. . . . What*
> *ever the mind can conceive and believe the mind can*
> *achieve.*

When Carnegie approached Hill about creating the first practical philosophy of personal success, Hill had limiting beliefs.

Hill told Carnegie that he was the wrong person because of his youth, lack of education, and finances. Carnegie responded with a lecture that became the turning point of Hill's life, telling Hill there was great power under his command, a power greater than poverty, lack of education, greater than all fears combined. It is the power to take dominion of one's own mind and wisely direct it. This power, Carnegie furthered, is the greatest gift of the Creator, because it is the only thing giving man the complete and unchallengeable right of control and direction.

I began studying Hill's masterpiece (*The Law of Success*) at 19. While reading it I wrote down and concentrated on three goals: earning $100,000 or more per year (which at the time seemed outrageous), discovering my purpose, and buying a new convertible sports car. By 20, within one year of declaring my goals, I had realized all three. Over the years I've realized countless victories, which is why I know you can too. The previous chapter gave you the *formula* to direct your mind, regardless of circumstance, to consciously create your vision. This chapter helps you integrate it. Through stories and suggestions, your mind will be stimulated, evoking empowering states that support you in consciously creating your dream life.

WE ARE ALL ENDOWED
WITH SUPERHUMAN STRENGTH

One of my dear friends is a superhuman athlete. His name is Dr. Nick. One day while we were having dinner, he said, "I'm going to break the world record for strength and endurance next week. Do you want to emcee the event?"

"Sure," I said. In this competition, he would alternate lifting twenty-five- to forty-pound dumbbells in each hand, from the hip, into a curl, and then an overhead press, for one straight hour with zero breaks. I asked him, "Tell me how you break these records." He shared his success formula. He had a strategy that included specific nutrition (he was mostly vegan); precise hydration; ideal body temperature while lifting; a knowledge of what intervals he would count in; the amount of weight he wanted to lift, by when; and how he would focus his concentration. He had trained and already broken the record in his mind countless times. When I arrived at the gym the night of the event, Nick was in the zone. I looked at him and instantly knew he would win. That night, at 52 years old, Nick broke the world record with 1,974 lifts, totaling 50,640 pounds, beating the previous record of 41,025 pounds by almost 10,000 pounds!

When I asked what inspired him, he said, "Believing in one's ability to surpass human limits, and raising money for children with autism."

The mental and emotional state you emanate when formulating your goal will be the state in which your goal returns to you. Nick had absolute certainty he would break the world record. The night of the event, there were raging fires throughout Southern California. I remember having a difficult time driving to the location because of the smoke. Many experts urged him to postpone the competition, saying it would damage his lungs to perform this feat under such unfavorable conditions. But Nick would not listen to naysayers. He observed *what is* without attachment and focused on victory. His state was unstoppable—and the Universe echoed back.

Summoning an empowered state is essential to mastering the Ten-Step Formula for Conscious Creation that you learned in the previous chapter. Why? Because this formula works! It does not play favorites. Whatever vibe you emanate when using this formula is the vibe that gets embedded into your goal, and it's the vibe that echoes back. The Universe is just. It is not possible to work this formula in a state of doubt and attract power. This means if someone applies all the steps, but in doing so has doubt, then, depending on the degree of doubt intensity, it gets embedded into the goal as a *doubt form*, and doubt will boomerang back. What you attract reflects the dominant thoughts of your mind.

A centered state allows you to manifest your vision. Neutrality frees you from the ego's entrapments, ensuring you are not manipulated by false desires. When your mind is calm and detached, you create the appropriate conditions for divine energy to flow unobstructed. As an acorn requires proper conditions—fertile soil, sunshine, abundant fresh water, clean air—to evolve into a mighty oak tree and fulfill its potential, we also *thrive* in the proper environment.

When you are in a neutral and present state, you can more readily discern the wisest choice. It becomes obvious in the moment. Disempowering emotions poison the mind and cloud vision, leading to mis-creation. In Buddhism, the three primary *mind poisons* (or *kleshas*)—ignorance, anger, and greed—are the root cause of suffering, which facilitate mis-creation. Ignorance is primary because it leads to the other two. But ignorance is not a substantial thing. It is the absence of awareness; it's being "in effect." Therefore, if you experience doubt, do not apply the formula just yet. First expand your awareness. One way to accomplish this is to go for a walk into nature and allow your vision to expand into the periphery as you breathe a little deeper. Feel the love you have for Mother Earth. Practice mantra. Clear your mind by imagining a wave of purifying water cascading through your consciousness. Then call forth an empowered state, such as poise, bravery, or any mind-set that most resonates for the situation.

Here's a story of how I transformed doubt and consciously created my reality.

FAITH LET ME GO

After nearly five years on the road, traveling to a different city every two months and breaking sales records for Tony Robbins, it was time for a change. Although I loved my work, I was tired of traveling, and I didn't see the kind of growth I desired within the organization. I had no idea where Spirit would lead me, but intuitively I knew change was essential for my evolution. I met with my manager and explained my desire for a graceful and purposeful exit over a two-month period. I figured I'd discern my next step while giving the company ample opportunity to replace me. To ease the transition, I offered to train new team members. A couple days after my meeting, I received a phone call from an executive at the company—who, as fate would have it, was named Faith. She thanked me for my contribution and informed me my transition would be immediate. I had no idea where I would live, what I would drive, or what I would do. But *faith* let me go.

My thoughts began reeling, and for a moment I was lost in chaos. *How could this happen?* I thought. I felt kicked to the curb. For the first time since running away from home, my neck became stiff and pinned itself to my shoulder. I'd come a long way, but in that moment, I felt vulnerable, empty, homeless, and tribeless.

The next morning I drove to the chiropractor, knowing I couldn't figure anything out until my body was in alignment. The chiropractor examined my back and said, "Your spine looks like a question mark."

"That's because I'm questioning everything," I responded. After my adjustment, I drove to the beach and went for a long walk, doing my best to transmute hurt feelings, decipher my own sad perceptions, and figure out what to do next.

I sat on a rock and cried, watching the waves crash. I began practicing japa, a spiritual discipline involving the repetition of a mantra (sacred sounds with transformative power) or a divine name of power. I learned japa from an Indian maharishi in New York City. He guided me in transmuting negative thought forms by chanting *Om* and *Ah*. It's impossible to have a negative thought and vibe on *Om* in the same instant. In his particular lineage, he instructed students to chant *Om* in the evenings with gratitude, and *Ah* in the mornings with creative intention. He said many of the holy names of God have the sound vibration "*Ah*"—*God (sounds like gAHd), KrishnAH, YAHweh, BrAHmAH, RamAH, AHdonai, BuddAH, IshwAHrAH, AllAH, ShivAH, RAH, JehovAH, MessiAH* (note: all God names spelled phonetically).

God has a thousand names; or rather,
he is nameless. We may worship or pray to him
by whichever name that pleases us.
All worship the same Spirit.

—MAHATMA GANDHI

I sat in lotus position, praying for clarity, and whispering *Ah* from the depth of my being. After some time I began feeling calm, then peace. My breath deepened and my posture straightened as I continued chanting for hours, pausing for moments to simply witness and allow the healing power of nature to wash over me. I realized that all the while I had ups and downs, twists and turns, the rock I was sitting on, simply—*was*. Life *is*.

Through my meditation the pain dissolved into emptiness. I sat in silence . . . in the void. In the stillness an inner voice spoke, "Decide on the next step; you don't need to see the full picture yet." Instantly an image of a red Mercedes-Benz flashed in my mind, along with the thought, *I need a new car, that's step one. Then I need a place to live, that's step two. But first, a car.*

I took a deep breath and formulated a crystal-clear image in my mind of me careening down the California coast in a brand-new Benz, wind blowing through my hair. I was looking through my own eyes, driving my new car. I could see the richness of the colors, hear the revving of the engine, feel the grip of the steering wheel beneath my fingers, and smell the salt in the air. I declared, "I am *NiurkAH*, and this is my car."

With a newfound sense of enthusiasm, I stood up to go. As I turned, I saw a man who apparently had been watching me. He walked over and asked, "Were you talking to God?"

"Yes," I said.

He replied, "I talk to God too." He was holding an expensive pair of binoculars, which he handed to me and said, "These are for you." I was astonished. He said, "Please take them; they are a gift, that you may always see clearly the truth beyond appearances."

"Thank you," I said in utter awe, holding them close to my heart.

"Can I share a story with you?" he asked.

"Yes," I said. He spoke gently, lovingly. He told me a story of two hounds, one black and one white, who would regularly battle. And how there was a man who always knew which dog would win. His tale confounded me. *Why were the dogs battling?* I thought, but I listened. "Do you know why he knew which dog would win?" he asked.

"No," I said.

"Because each night he would look to see which dog the owner fed." I was confused. *Am I missing something here?* I thought. *I'm not getting the punch line.* He said, "You have two dogs inside of you. One is of the light, the other of the shadow; the one you feed will win. Today I saw you feed the light, and I am here to tell you the light will prevail. Keep feeding the light." With that, he turned and walked away, leaving me bewildered and with a new pair of binoculars. I realized I didn't catch his name—maybe it was Dog spelled backward.

I snapped out of my hypnotic trance. *That was a trip,* I thought. As I looked at the gift, I knew it was a sign I was on the right path. On the way back to my apartment, I stopped and bought a bunch of moving boxes and shipping tape. I packed up my books and belongings until midnight. Then, before collapsing on the couch, I chanted *Om* in gratitude for the revelation and connection I made with the mysterious man.

I was at a crossroads, feeling called to traverse unknown realms of my being, to discover aspects of my self that would grant me the wisdom to set my new course. Inspiration and direction came in the form of a man with binoculars, who reminded me to see with enlightened eyes. In this light my challenge became a gift.

The next morning I decided to go get my new car. There was

just one challenge. Since I had been making a nice six-figure income and driving corporate rental cars for almost five years, I had zero credit. The lavish lifestyle, the world travel, the five-star hotels, the fine dining, the shopping sprees . . . all paid for with cash. Saving money was not a priority, because I knew *One day I would make billions. So why save now?* I thought it was better to enjoy my money while I was young, which in retrospect was not the wisest choice.

After assessing my situation, I considered alternative ways to achieve my goal. I began stretching the boundaries of my thinking, asking myself questions: *How can I align with the general manager of a car dealership and creatively position myself to drive off the lot with a brand-new car that I love today?* The answer came immediately—*Barter for my corporate training services* (which didn't yet exist).

I chanted *Ah*, put on my suit, and departed for automobile row in Los Angeles. Although I wanted a Mercedes-Benz, the internal representation in my mind was *Supremely specific*, which means I was clear on my outcome—manifesting a brand-new car that I love today—and not attached to how it would show up, allowing the Universe to bring me the essence of my desire in whatever way reflected divine order. I organized my thoughts and strategized, ensuring I had more than one way to achieve my goal. Plan B was Porsche. Plan C was BMW. I was ready to change my approach if necessary. I was certain I would not leave automobile row without my new car. I was resolved. I would not accept defeat; I would not be denied. It was a unique balance interweaving strategy and surrender. The key was clarity of intent and nonattachment, of relinquishing lust for result.

I drove to the dealership in the corporate car I had to

return in two days. While driving, I accessed the internal representation I had created while sitting on the rock at the beach. *I am cruising in my new red Mercedes-Benz. Looking through my own eyes, it's happening in the now.* I was clear I wanted a red Mercedes, but I could easily have transformed it into a black Porsche or a silver Beemer or something even better. I was flexible. The essence of the goal was clear, bright, and crisp. I was sitting in the driver's seat, looking through the windshield of my new reality. Although it was happening in my imagination, it was "real." I could observe everything around me panoramically as I cruised down Pacific Coast Highway. In my mind, the deal was done, and I amplified the feeling of absolute certainty. With my head and heart aligned, I declared:

> *I am grateful I materialized my new car instantly and properly today. So it is.*

I pulled into Downtown L.A. Motors Mercedes-Benz. As I walked to the showroom floor, I asked myself empowering questions: *How may I serve? How can I communicate with the general manager so he knows for a fact I am the most qualified person on the planet to help him achieve his goals?*

Remember the story of the Lion and the Squirrel from chapter 3? It was the Lion, the top salesman, who greeted me at the front door. He escorted me to the general manager's office, and with a growly grin expressed his enthusiasm about our potential partnership. The GM and I developed a sweet connection. I liked him and was inspired to work with him and his team. We talked about his business objectives, challenges, and vision.

I explained how I would help him achieve his goals and then proposed a barter agreement.

In my heart of hearts, I knew I would sign a deal that day, either with him or someone else, but I wanted it to be him. He was my first choice, and I told him so. We talked, laughed, and negotiated for hours. Our meeting ended with a handshake, consummating a barter agreement for a one-year lease worth over $1,500 a month for a brand-new red Mercedes-Benz in exchange for my corporate training services not yet formulated. The GM and I became friends, and in less than one year, the dealership exceeded its sales objectives. This opened the door for me to work with several other Mercedes-Benz dealers, including Fletcher Jones Motor Cars, who rose to be the number-one Mercedes-Benz dealer in the world and number-two dealer of all makes and models in the United States, increasing their sales by 10 to 20 percent each year that I facilitated training and led initiatives with their leaders.

LAW OF ATTRACTION:
YOU ATTRACT YOUR VIBRATIONAL MATCH

OM (ALSO SPELLED AUM)

I chanted *Om* and *Ah* on the beach that day, united with the Creative Powers. I was in such a high-vibrational state through empowering questions, affirmations, visualizations, meditations, and mantra that doubt dissolved. My vision was accomplished in the unseen realms. Then I spoke my vision into existence, and it became so.

The law of attraction teaches that you are a vibrational being, and through your vibration, you create your reality. Let me explain a little more.

The law of attraction is grounded in the law of vibration: everything in the manifest universe vibrates, and like vibrations attract. When your vibration is high and pure, you attract people and experiences matching that vibe. You create your reality through your *vibe*. What you get is what you give.

When someone walks into a room, you feel their vibe. You instantly sense that person's mood. You see it in her body language, hear it in her voice, and feel it in the atmosphere around you, even if she doesn't speak a word. Thoughts create ambience. Some people seem to dominate a room with their energy, while others fade into the background. Some people seem naturally adept at creating loving, peaceful vibes, while others convey energies of tension or angst. You have the power to walk into any room and set the tone through your intention and vibration.

There is a concept in physics called "resonance," which states that when two frequencies are aligned it makes the vibration stronger, generating more power. You can discover this yourself with a brief experiment. Open a piano and pluck the C string. Observe what happens. All of the C strings in the piano vibrate! The one that vibrates the most is the one closest to the one plucked. And so it is with you. Your vibration influences life all around you.

Have you ever noticed how sometimes a particular song comes on the radio and it speaks to you? Every cell in your body dances and responds. It's as though you feel it in your bones. You are in resonance. Other times you hear that same song and it doesn't move you at all. In those moments, you aren't resonating with the song's frequency. This is the basis of the law of attraction. You attract into your experience what resonates with your vibration. When you shift your vibration, you shift what materializes in the world around you. One way to accomplish this is through intoning or chanting. Pick a name of power, any one that resonates with you. It can be your own name, a holy name, or the sacred sound Om. Sit or stand with your spine erect and both feet flat on the ground. Then intone or chant the name. Allow the vibration to permeate your being, and notice how it elevates how you feel.

When you're authentically in resonance with your goal, you don't need to look at it every day. You can release it, knowing it is accomplished. Many of us were taught to write down goals and look at them daily. This is only partially effective. If someone writes down a goal while experiencing doubt, then a doubt form could be embedded into that goal. Only look at your goal if looking at it delights you.

Consider this: What is one area of your life where you naturally succeed? Let's say you know with absolute certainty you're an amazing parent. If you believe this with every cell in your being, you likely don't have to set a ton of goals around it. You don't need to look in the mirror and affirm, "I'm a great parent. I'm a great parent. I'm a great parent." You don't need affirmations for the things you already know to be true. Before you declare your goal, create the knowing that it is already done, and it will be.

IIIIIIIIIIIIIIIIIIIIIII   **SUPREME BONUS**   IIIIIIIIIIIIIIIIIIIIIIIII

Invoking Intuitive Intelligence
Through the Gayatri Mantra

When I first journeyed to Bali, I was recovering from a leg break and
I had a limp. I was rolled out of the airport in a wheelchair. After
vibing on the Gayatri mantra for one week and nurturing myself, I
was walking well and feeling more alive and grounded. This mantra
is Sanskrit, sounds angelic, and has great mystical powers, meaning
it elevates your vibration in a way that cannot be described with
words but must be experienced. The key to mantra is action, the
repetition (preferably silently or whispering) of these divine words
of power.

Sanskrit prayers have been recited and sung for millennia. Every
tradition has its own mantras and prayers. It's a good idea to practice
the ones that resonate with you. Studies declare a person has approx-
imately sixty thousand thoughts per day, and many of these thoughts
repeat. All thought is creative, and you think quite often. Mantra is a
holy vibe that replaces scattered, unconscious thinking with sacred
sounds of power. This transference of energy creates fertile ground
for something new to be born.

Remember, mantra is vibration, so don't get caught up in the
intellectual translation of letters or words. Mystics know the mantra
itself reveals its secrets to you when practiced. I've studied many
English translations of the Gayatri mantra and have not found one
meaning that describes its immense power. In my experience it
activates your intuitive intelligence. Here's my best translation of
the Gayatri mantra:

With deep love and reverence, we meditate
on the glory of the Supreme Being
who creates and sustains this Universe.
May this Being enlighten our minds.

Whisper it now, and again in the next hour and the next. Feel its power. Discover its magic and allow it to bless and evolve your life. Gayatri mantra in Sanskrit:

ॐ

OM

भूर्भुवः स्वः

BHUR BHUVAH SUVAHA

तत् सवितुर् वरेण्यं

TAT SAVITUR VARENIYAM

भर्गो देवस्य धीमहि

BHARGO DEVASYA DHEEMAHI

धियो यो नः प्रचोदयात्

DHIYO YO NAH PRACHODAYATH

14

ASK AND YOU SHALL RECEIVE

Your life mirrors the quality of the questions you ask. Questions direct your focus. They determine what you perceive, attract, and materialize in a universe of infinite possibility.

The greatest minds of our time have enriched our world by asking imaginative questions. The most significant technological advances in history originated with a question. Questions open portals to previously unimagined realms. Einstein came to his theories of relativity by contemplating, *What would happen if I rode a beam of light?* Walt Disney asked, *How can I create the happiest place on Earth?* Steve Jobs began each day asking, *If today were the last day of my life, would I want to do what I am about to do today?* Questions guided these geniuses to discover, create, and gift our world with innovations that advanced our lives. Clearly, questions like these lead to radically different results than *What do I have to do today?*

Questions can be used to gather information, understand another's map of the world, develop rapport, clarify meaning, explore opportunities, direct focus, invoke empowering states, expand imagination, transform challenges, refine your vision, amplify your materializing power, and more. This chapter shows you how to wield questions to activate your potential. You will become more aware of the questions you ask yourself, and you will learn a formula to consciously craft empowering questions that call forth your brilliance.

Throughout history many gurus, teachers, and enlightened masters chose to teach only students who asked well-formed questions. A single well-formed question can bring the seemingly impossible within reach. Questions invite a response. They can shatter old paradigms and open entirely new ways of thinking and being. Once a question is properly formulated, the answer is within reach.

When you are ready to receive the answers, they come.

I remember several defining moments in my life when contemplating *one* question transformed everything, shifting my focus from problems to wonder and possibility. Here's one of those moments.

ONE QUESTION TRANSFORMS EVERYTHING

Long ago, there was a time when I felt alone and aimless. Looking back, I recall asking myself a flood of questions that directed my attention toward experiences I didn't want. I was unconsciously invoking low feelings with questions like *Why is this happening? What am I going to do? What's the point? What's wrong with me? What's wrong with people? What's wrong with the world? How did I get on this planet?* And guess what? My life mirrored the vibration of those questions. During that time I looked around and saw mostly chaos, struggle, and disappointment. My questions were shaping my *map of reality*. Let me explain.

I was 19 and working in the seminar business (before Tony Robbins). The owner of the first company fired me. The second company filed for bankruptcy and shorted me an $8,000 pay-check. At the same time, I discovered my boyfriend sleeping with another girl, which he later explained was because she was prettier and skinnier. I was living in a Marriott hotel room in Hartford, Connecticut, until I got kicked out for accidentally almost setting my room on fire with a burning candle. Feeling displaced and weary from dodging obstacles, I knew I had to make a change. I had nowhere to go, no plan, very little money, and no idea what to do next.

While wallowing in that lonely hotel room, I phoned my friend Dave. I wanted direction. Dave and I met when his brother hired me for my first job in the seminar world. Dave bought me my first pair of business boots when I couldn't afford them. I liked Dave and valued his guidance.

I moaned to Dave about the injustices befalling me, how miserable and inept the world appeared, and how I couldn't find my way out of this mess. I felt jaded. But Dave didn't buy into my story. He waited for me to finish ranting, then with a stoic voice asked, "If you could be anywhere in the world right now, where would you be?"

"Anywhere?" I asked. The question made me stop for a moment. What did "anywhere" mean? Where would I be if I could be *anywhere*? My mind traveled toward the infinite center of the cosmos. I let it whirl around the globe.

Then Dave said, "Yes, anywhere."

I responded, "I would be hiking naked, in the desert, by myself!" The words snapped off my tongue like a cracking whip.

There was a pause. Dave spoke: "If that's where you wanted to be, then that's where you'd be." Dead silence . . . followed by a dial tone. Dave had hung up on me. I stared at the phone in shock.

Dave's words rang in my ears like daggers on my consciousness, cutting through the bullshit excuses. In an instant I realized he was right. If I wanted to be hiking naked in the desert by myself, then that's where I would be. I had choice. And the profundity of that awareness sent shudders through my destiny. The next day I packed my car, bought a map of the United States, and drove straight for the largest desert I could find—the Grand Canyon.

Sometimes great gifts for our evolution come wrapped in strange packages. When my former boss went bankrupt without paying me, he nonchalantly remarked, "It's just business, kid. But you can keep all those audiocassettes." I inherited a big, black storage trunk full of audiocassettes, covering topics such as motivation, influence, leadership, psychology of success, NLP, hypnosis, and sales. I slipped the first cassette into my black convertible Mitsubishi Spyder Eclipse turbo and started driving. I listened to those cassettes over and over, as though my life depended on it. In a way, it did.

Driving through Navajo and Apache counties, the Petrified Forest, the Painted Desert, and the colorful badlands of Arizona was spiritually nourishing. I would pull over and walk through the dunes toward the sunset, which beamed orange hues through vast expansive skies. I hiked, witnessing life, while snakes hunted mice in the twilight hours between day and evening. I would sit on fossilized wood, with lizards, and contemplate, feeling frozen in space-time. Sitting in silence, I gazed at flickering campfires while hearing the subtle hum of native flutes whistling within the trees. I observed thoughts and wrote in my journal, finding great solace transforming pain into poetry:

Heed!
Choose never need.
Only then will you be freed
From ignorance and greed,
Or a dogmatic creed,
Designed to blind you as you plead.
See every moment contains a seed
Of opportunity that can lead
To newfound success at lightning speed
Because your true essence will bleed
On each moment-to-moment deed.

Dave's one question awakened a new possibility. I'd been stuck, looping in my own self-imposed perceptions, unable to conceive a way out. One question reminded me that I had *choice.* I had the freedom to choose what to do with my life, how to be, where to go, who to be with. The possibilities were endless. Even though I could hear a little voice inside my head saying, *Wait! This is crazy! What are you thinking? You can't just drive twenty-five hundred miles to the desert without a plan!* Those thoughts became irrelevant. I watched them come and go like the ebb and flow of the tide. I didn't identify with them. Instead I wondered where they originated and if they were even mine. I was tired of struggling; I was ready to let go. I whispered to myself, *With faith the size of a mustard seed I can move mountains.* As this affirmation rolled off my lips, I smiled. I felt energy in those words lifting my spirit and deepening my breath. I knew I was in a doorway between dimensions. This was a defining moment. I was at a crossroads, and I was ready.

I arrived in Flagstaff, Arizona, just south of the snowcapped

San Francisco Peaks, and negotiated a deal on a studio apartment by the college. I bought myself the basics: one cup, one
plate, one fork, one towel, one pillow, and one sheet.

The desert gave me a soothing sense of adventure. Suspense
and freedom beckoned me to explore the limits of my humanity, the depths of my own soul and unfolding potential. For six
weeks I hiked alone in the desert, following this evolutionary
impulse wherever it led me. I was alert, and receptive, and asking different questions now: *What's most important to me? What
am I inspired to do? What do I want to learn? Whom do I want to
play and create with? What am I grateful for? What is the wisest
choice? How can I manifest a miracle right now?*

These were radically different questions than the ones I
had been asking just weeks before! These questions were opening an entirely new awareness. My entire reality transformed
almost instantly! I used questions to catapult myself into a new
realm of existence. Here, I had choice.

After six weeks I wanted contact with civilization. I called
my friend Jeff from a payphone. We had been coworkers at the
last company, and when they went bankrupt, he went to work
for Robbins Research International (RRI, aka the Anthony
Robbins Company). Jeff relayed to me a discussion he had had
with the managers at RRI about a "kid" who had broken all
these sales records. He said they wanted to hire me. So I packed
my bags to begin the next phase of my adventure.

Questions became a portal for progress. I would drive for
hours to businesses to deliver my presentation. On the way I
would stimulate my mind with a sea of empowering questions:
*How may I serve? What is my ultimate outcome for this meeting?
How specifically will I know when I achieve it? How can I connect*

with the decision maker? How can I understand what's most important to him? How can I inspire action? How can I authentically connect with each person present?

Asking myself empowering questions became a ritual I used to align my focus, language, and physiology with my vision. This practice supported me in becoming even more present and clear in my communication, which improved my relationships and skyrocketed my results.

QUESTIONS SUMMON THEIR MATCH

The important thing is not to stop questioning.
Curiosity has its own reason for existing.

—ALBERT EINSTEIN

Questions cause us to seek, expand, and learn. As humans we are growth-seeking beings. Questions open the way for us to explore beyond the boundaries of our previous thinking.

You can formulate a question to bring you what you want, like a heat-seeking missile encoded to search for a specific target. As you continue consciously crafting questions, the appropriate resources will appear, often seemingly out of the ether. Questions have manifesting power. They attract things to you, bringing people and experiences into your life. Questions sift through infinite possibilities and summon their vibrational match. Used unconsciously, they can bring unwanted experiences. Used intelligently, they pave the way for conscious creation.

What will happen in your life as you ask quality questions

that call forth your brilliance and presuppose success? What if you only asked questions you wanted the answer to? Mastering the art of consciously crafting questions grants you tremendous power.

Let's explore the power of questions from a neurological perspective. Remember the RAS, or reticular activating system, we discussed in chapter 7? It's the part of your brain that tells you what to notice.

QUESTIONS STIMULATE THE RAS
TO ATTRACT WHAT YOU WANT

Asking questions is a way to stimulate the RAS to find what you seek. We live in a universe of infinite possibility that responds to our thoughts. But infinite possibility is too much information for the human nervous system to absorb. Therefore, it's necessary to sift through the chaos (that which precedes form) and receive only the most important bits. Otherwise, we experience sensory overload, like trying to download the entire Internet.

Behavior can be subconscious, meaning that a person's actions can emerge automatically or without conscious awareness. One of the prime directives of the subconscious mind is *it follows clear, concise orders*. The subconscious mind is also more amenable to suggestion than to direct commands. Asking yourself questions can be more inviting than telling yourself what to do. Through questions you can program the RAS to sort through data and provide specific discoveries. Asking empowering questions causes you to attract allies and resources even when you are not actively thinking about them. You don't need to *know the answer* to your question. Simply ask with sincerity and certainty that an answer will come. And it will.

If you believe, you will receive
whatever you ask for in prayer.

—MATTHEW 21:22

What questions have you been asking? Get curious. Your observation (the observer effect) and declaration (Logos) influence what shows up in your life. Whatever you believe and call forth through your questions *will be*! You create as you speak. Imagine continually asking unlimited reality questions, such as *What is one thing I can do right now that will elevate every area of my life?* What will those questions attract? What previously deleted opportunities will you notice or envision?

THE FORMULA FOR CRAFTING EMPOWERING QUESTIONS

Empowering questions are consciously crafted questions that you ask yourself (or others) to inspire affirmative action toward a clear and desirable aim.

Asking empowering questions is important because questions direct your focus, which determines what you attract and manifest. All thought is creative. Thinking entails the process of asking and answering your own questions within your own mind. You do this already! Your life reflects the quality of the questions you ask. When you elevate your questions, you elevate your entire experience of reality. Imagine having a simple formula to craft questions that activate your higher intelligence, strengthen your purpose, and wisely direct your focus toward your desired aim. Here it is! Use the following three-step formula to build questions that inspire and empower *you* to live your epic life.

THE THREE-STEP FORMULA FOR CRAFTING EMPOWERING QUESTIONS

1. Begin with *how, what,* or *who.*
2. State in the *affirmative,* moving toward what you want.
3. Build momentum with words like *right now, while,* and *even more.*

Step 1

Start your empowering question with *how, what,* or *who.* These words set the stage for understanding and success. Starting a question with *why* can more easily lead to philosophical conversation or possibly amplify problems. For example: *Why is this happening?* If you use *why,* be sure it uplifts: *Why am I inspired to accomplish this?* Questions beginning with *why* can invoke a strong sense of purpose, but if used unconsciously, *why* questions can lead to downward spiral. Be aware. Begin your empowering question with *how, what,* or *who.*

Step 2

State your question in the affirmative. Be sure your language is flowing in the direction you want to go, *toward* your vision.

This means state what you *want*, not what you *don't want*. What do you want to create or experience? Let's suppose you have an important decision to make. You could ask, *What is the wisest choice? What is most important in the context of this decision? Having made this choice, how will I feel?*

Here's an example of what does *not* work. Let's say someone asks: "How can I not be such a procrastinator?" Consider what this question presupposes. The person may be trying to motivate herself to get things done. But the problem is, the question reinforces an old pattern and identity. We live in an attraction-based universe, so placing attention on not wanting something draws it nearer. It would be wiser to focus on having a clear direction.

One of the interesting things about the brain is that it doesn't process negatives. Meaning: if you tell someone *not* to look for something, they must look for it *before* they cannot look for it! Play along for a moment. Don't think of the color red. What are you thinking about right now? I bet you're thinking about red! Now, don't think of a blue tree. What are you thinking of right now? Before you can "not" think about something, you think about it first. Don't think of an octopus . . . on a unicycle . . . with a party hat on—think of anything but that! Now you may be thinking, *Gee thanks, Niurka! Now I've got octopus on the brain!*

This is why it's important to choose words wisely. Your words stimulate your RAS to find what you speak. So what is a more empowering question than *How can I not be such a procrastinator?* A more affirmative, results-oriented question could be: *How can I be more focused on accomplishing my top three results for the day?* Or *What's the best use of my time right now?*

Or *How inspired and empowered will I feel once this is accomplished?*

Once, when I taught this formula in a corporation, one customer service representative's "empowering" question was "How can I be more tolerant with customers who are jerks?" I could see he was seeking a solution, but exasperation clouded his vision. He was speaking from his experience; however, his question directed his focus toward more of what he *didn't* want.

What if he could create an entirely new experience for himself and his customers, simply by elevating his questions? What could happen if he shifted his language to the affirmative: *How can I genuinely connect with this person? How can I understand what specifically is most important to him? How can I honor his experience while clearly communicating our policy, so we both feel great at the end of this call? How can I resolve his challenge right now and exceed his expectations? How can I brighten his day? How can I bring all of my attention to this present moment?* If this rep asks himself these questions throughout the day, he'll have more fun at work, and his capacity for facilitating harmonious interactions will improve. He will become more productive and enjoy a richer life.

In the sea of possibilities, the potential for creating favorable contexts of communication and understanding is as infinite as the waves on the ocean.

Step 3

Build momentum with words like *right now, while,* or *even more.* Consider how these few words can change the energy of a question. We'll start with a basic question. Ask yourself, *How can I be focused?*

If you add *even more*, what happens to the question *How can I be even more focused?* It presupposes you *already are* focused and directs your energy toward amplifying your concentration. What if you asked, *How can I be even more focused right now?* The question brings your attention to the present moment, harnessing and directing your power. Notice how this question elicits a different feeling in your neurology.

Here's another example: *How can I be healthy and fit?*

By adding *even more*, the question becomes: *How can I be even more healthy and fit?* It assumes you *already are* healthy and fit. The statement is present tense, moving you toward health and fitness in the moment. But what if someone is nowhere close to feeling healthy and fit? Adding *even more* won't work! It will be a totally false statement prompting a person's brain to say, *Yeah, right! Who are you kidding?* It's important to begin with a congruent presupposition that inspires you toward the direction you want to go. For example, a person committed to optimum fitness, who feels a long way off, can begin with questions like *What healthy, delicious, and nutritious choices are available to me now? How can I be even more aware of the health existing within every cell of my body right now? What exercise can I enjoy today to strengthen my body? Who do I know that is a health/nutrition/fitness expert who can support me?* These questions form a bridge leading from one level of thinking to another realm.

If we add *right now*, how does that change the dynamic? The question *How can I be even more healthy and fit right now?* becomes *in* the present. It's not something you are planning to accomplish in the future; it's happening *now*. An answer to the first question could be "Go to the gym four times per week!" However, the answer to the second question may be, "Straighten your posture and smile!" Simply adding *right now* to the question causes your brain to find an answer immediately. If you don't specify a time, you may be eternally waiting! Notice the difference: *How can I feel inner peace?* versus *How can I tune into the inner peace within me right now?* Inserting *right now* takes the question out of the theoretical and into the practical and actionable. An answer to the first question could be "Well, I need to quit my job, go to the wilderness, meditate a lot, and then experience inner peace." Whereas the answer to the second question could be "As I inhale a conscious breath and gently remind myself how blessed I am, I know peace." Adding *while* can expand the question to include more specific and inspiring choices: *How can I be even more lean, healthy, and fit right now, while savoring foods I love?* With this one word *while*, you can create questions that include *all* kinds of possibilities, *while* allowing the Universe to delight you in even more fantastical ways than you ever imagined.

I realize these questions may appear a bit long-winded. Certainly, they may sound unusual. However, they create conditions supporting you in achieving your ultimate dream life. So get playful and creative, and trust the process. Remember, it's in our nature to ask questions. We do this throughout the day, often without thinking about it. Now we are asking consciously. The key is to craft questions that inspire, while wholeheartedly anticipating answers, with zero attachment as to how they will manifest. Relax, know the answer will come, and it will!

Now that you have the Formula for Crafting Empowering Questions, let's fine-tune.

FINE-TUNING QUESTIONS:
DISTINCTIONS MAKE ALL THE DIFFERENCE

Now I'll share two sets of questions, each of which could be asked within the same scenario. Notice how shifting the language changes the viewpoint and leads to radically different results:

Why is it so difficult to get ahead?

versus

What can I do right now to accomplish _____?

Or . . .

What if it doesn't work?

versus

What value can I bring to this project right now to ensure the highest result is achieved?

Contemplate the differences between the questions above. The first question in each set focuses on the problem and the *absence* of something. The second question focuses on the opportunity and the *presence* of something. The distinction here is huge, because we receive what we focus on most.

BE SUPREMELY SPECIFIC

Details are important! Be specific when asking questions, just not too specific. You want to remain open to infinite possibilities surrounding you.

Make everything as simple as possible,
but not simpler.

—ALBERT EINSTEIN

If someone asks the question *How can I attract abundance?*
she may think it's an empowering question—but not necessarily.
The inherent vagueness of the question becomes the challenge.
We live in a universe of abundance. There's an abundance of
sand in the Sahara, an abundance of traffic in Los Angeles, an
abundance of stars in the heavens. What kind of abundance
are you asking for—specifically? In a universe of infinite possibility, unfocused questions attract nonspecific results. Focused
attention commands manifestations. There is a big difference
between focusing on abundance versus focusing on materializing an actual sum of money by a specific date or sooner.

When you craft your question, you want to be specific in
intention and nonattached to a particular outcome. You want
to see, hear, and feel the essence of what you desire in your
mind, without becoming attached to the form through which
it will manifest. As with the Ten-Step Formula for Conscious
Creation, you want to be *Supremely specific.*

A fine line exists between being specific and being *too* specific. I once had a woman in one of my courses who was single
and wished to meet her life's partner. I asked her to describe
what she wanted, and she gave me an exact list: "He's handsome, over six feet tall, with dark hair. He has a good job and
makes six figures, but he's not a workaholic. He lives within
ten miles of me and loves to cook. He's never been married,

doesn't have children yet, but wants at least two, a boy and a girl. His parents are still married. He doesn't watch football or drink beer, but he does like a glass of wine every now and then, but never more than one or two in an evening. He's an amazing lover, and doesn't snore. Oh yeah, and he loves to snuggle . . . all night long." Then she said in a giddy tone and with a smile, "His name is Todd." It's possible this woman could have met the perfect partner, reflecting the essence of her priorities in a man—but what if his name was Francisco and he was five foot nine? She could miss the connection (and the door of opportunity). She could be so focused on her list that she may dismiss men with great relationship potential.

This is an extreme and silly example, certainly. She may have been open to meeting Francisco, but the point is, the brain is programmed to find what you're looking for. If you're too identified, you risk getting tunnel vision. It's essential to be clear about *what you want* and take action, *while* allowing the Universe to orchestrate the arrival of your ultimate goal.

ANSWERS ABOUND

Answers surround you. Any question you ask has an answer, awaiting discovery. Every challenge you experience contains within it the solution for an emerging possibility, one sparking evolution. However, if someone is too narrowed in focus or anchored in a particular frame of mind, he won't see the possibilities.

I once had a student in a weeklong course share a story about trusting answers to appear. A day before sharing, Steven had been searching with all his might for answers to a few important questions about his life. He felt confused but was committed to understand. Steven knew the answers were just around the corner. Still, he found it challenging to relax, because the answers weren't immediately obvious to him. I told him to trust the process, get a good night's sleep, then return to class tomorrow. "The answers will come," I said.

The next day he came to class and shared. Arriving home after class, Steven realized he had lost one of his contact lenses. Panicked, and not knowing what to do, he called his wife, who was out of town. After speaking with her, he regained his composure and began retracing his steps, as his wife suggested. He looked in his car, on the seat, under the seat, on the floor, on the dashboard, on the steering wheel, in the glove box. With escalating anxiety Steven searched inside his house. He looked in the kitchen and in the fridge. Then he traced his steps backward through the garage, on the pathway to his car, looked under his car, then went back inside the house. Exasperated, Steven went to check the medicine cabinet for an extra set of contacts. While reaching to open the cabinet, he glanced in the mirror, and there, resting on the end of his nose, was his contact lens. It was literally right in front of his face.

Once you ask a question, be open to receive. Relax in the moment knowing that the answer is near. It's closer than you think.

QUESTIONS ABOUT QUESTIONS

Are you stimulated? Elevated? Aroused by the potency of questions? I encourage you to keep a journal and develop an ever-evolving list of your own empowering questions. See it as sacred ritual born from intent and love, unifying you with Supreme Intelligence.

Get curious about your questions. Are your questions formulated in the most inspiring way? Do they arouse your Supreme Influence? Once you've crafted an empowering question, contemplate using metaquestions (or questions about the questions) to discern if the question you crafted expresses your authentic intent while summoning your desires without attachment. As you ask yourself these metaquestions, listen to your body's responses.

Metaquestions

Metaquestions, or questions about questions, cause you to self-reflect, clarify your intent, and formulate precise language to bridge worlds and accomplish aims.

Here are examples of metaquestions you can ask to refine your questions.

What does my question presuppose? Does it evoke the highest within me? Does my question absolutely support my magnificence and what I envision? Does it inspire me and everyone involved? How does this question make me feel? If I were to receive the answer to this question instantly, how ready, open, and receptive am I to it? One hundred percent? On a scale from zero to ten, how powerful is this question in attracting what I want? (If it's not yet a ten, keep refining the question until every cell in your body becomes alive, energized, and pulled toward your vision.)

YOUR STATE PERMEATES YOUR QUESTION

Remember the story of how I promptly manifested the red Mercedes-Benz? I had a movie in my mind of the successful

outcome accomplished in advance. It was *Supremely specific.*
I embodied a physiology of certainty. Then I stood up, picked
up the phone, called the decision maker (the general manager
GM), and scheduled a face-to-face meeting. On the way to the
dealership, I infused my consciousness with purposeful questions,
summoning empowered states within myself before walking into
the showroom. I asked: *What is my ultimate outcome for this meeting? How specifically will I know when I achieve it? How can I create rapport quickly? How can I understand what specifically is most
important to the GM? How can I be even more present in my listening? What do I appreciate about the GM and his leadership? How can
I help him solve his biggest challenge? How can I understand what is
most important to him in aligning with a consultant, me? How can
I communicate in a way that inspires him to engage with me immediately? How can I create significant value for him right now? How
can I be even more articulate? How can I allow the Creative Powers
of the Universe to flow and speak through me? How can I manifest a
brand-new car on trade, instantly and properly today?*

By the time I walked into that establishment, I was oozing
Supreme Influence. Questions supported me in balancing the
force of my desire with my clear intent. These questions stimulated my RAS and elevated my vibe. I felt like a superhero. The
GM and I connected instantly and deeply. Within a few hours
we crafted an agreement matching our shared vision.

When you ask purposeful questions and are receptive,
you summon answers that exist in the field of all possibility.
Ask your question from the depth of your being and know
the answer will come. For weeks I meditated with a shaman
who illuminated the magical powers of speaking and asking questions, without words, from the infinite depth of one's
heart—*the space of stillness.* "This is how you commune with

Spirit," he said. Here the question and the answer become one. He also said, "This is how you and I can communicate via telepathy, because when we speak from the infinite space within our being, there is no time or space, only consciousness. When you want to call me, don't use a cell phone; call me from the infinite space within your heart, and I will hear you." That night we unexpectedly went to the temple. The air was cool and crisp. The stars were sparkling. My body felt frozen as I sat on the concrete floor in meditation. To comfort myself, I recited a line from the Bhagavad Gita, where Krishna says to Arjuna, "The one dear to me is neither affected by cold nor by heat." Committed to maintaining equilibrium, I allowed my consciousness to become the coldness itself. Finally, I offered a prayer from the depth of my heart asking for warmth. The next day the shaman gave me a fuzzy purple blanket.

Honor life and ask sincerely from your depths. An answer will come. Questions are a doorway to the expansion of Spirit in the human experience. Questions spark openings pioneering new ways of thinking and being. Purposeful questions properly guide attention and harmonize your life with divine order. They create possibility and summon their match. As soon as consciousness evolves to ask a particular question, a corresponding answer simultaneously becomes available in the field of potential. Similar to how every yang has a corresponding yin and every night a day, every question has an answer.

Through questions and observation, you can develop an intimate dialogue with life. Ask a question, then listen, watch, and feel. Omens will emerge in your awareness. The Universe will speak directly to you, offering symbols and signs so serendipitous it couldn't possibly be coincidence.

When you arrive at a crossroads, you can ask, *What is the most intelligent choice? Which path illuminates my purpose? Which choice leads to greater wisdom and understanding? Which choice will support me in realizing my ultimate vision? Is it wiser to go this way or that way? What would love do?* Ask and be still. Listen. Trust your intuition to guide you. By cultivating a sincere elevated inquiry, you commune with the Universe, as you would dialogue with a lover, trusted friend, or beloved teacher. The answer comes, and you realize you didn't ask for it, you invoked love.

It's sweet to ask a question for the sheer purpose of relating, without seeking a particular answer but rather for the utter joy, delight, and wonder of communing, knowing that at the highest level the question and the answer are inseparable, one and the same—*the question is the answer!* As the Sufi mystic poet Rumi said, "We are the mirror as well as the face in it."

This is how Devi, the feminine aspect of the Divine (also known as Shakti), asks her lover, Shiva, who is a major Hindu deity, to reveal the essence of the Supreme ultimate reality in the sacred tantric text Vijñāna Bhairava Tantra. Fully surrendered in love and the bliss of lovemaking, she melts into her lover as she asks:

> *O Shiva, what is your reality?*
> *What is this wonder-filled Universe?*
> *What constitutes seed?*
> *Who centers the universal wheel?*
> *What is this life beyond form pervading forms?*
> *How may we enter it fully, above space and time, names*
>   *and descriptions?*

Shiva does not give Devi an intellectual response, for the path to enlightenment through Tantra is not intellectual, rather it is experiential. Instead Shiva offers a technique that reveals the essence of what Devi is really asking. Devi's question needs no intellectual answer because she is living the answer. The answer is expressed through her surrender and love. She gives and receives in the same breath. There is no duality in Tantra because love transcends duality. This is a heart-to-heart talk, not a head-to-head discussion. The question and the answer both are present in a unified field of love. Yin and yang are two expressions of one reality.

Ultimately, this is the experience a Supreme inquiry leads to . . . the simultaneity of asking questions and receiving answers. This is grace—all is unfolding now as we relate in an intimate exchange with the world around us. Questions can be a form of lovemaking with the Universe.

The way you make love is the way
God will be with you.

—RUMI

THE ULTIMATE QUESTION

I want to know God's thoughts,
the rest are mere details.

—ALBERT EINSTEIN

You are one with the Supreme, and through stillness and purposeful questions you come closer to seeing with enlightened eyes, hearing with divine ears, feeling unconditional love, and knowing what Infinite Intelligence knows.

Now is the time to create your own questions to raise your vibration and invite an expanded understanding and a deeper sense of purpose.

Questions have the power to summon Infinite Intelligence, creativity, joy, and possibility. Open your heart and mind and craft the most inspiring questions to elevate every area of life!

Ask and it shall be given you,
seek and you shall find,
knock and it shall be opened unto you.

—MATTHEW 7:7

15

NAVIGATING FRAMES

The problem cannot be solved with the same level
of thinking that created it.

—ALBERT EINSTEIN

Above my fireplace rest two framed paintings. One is a mandala painted by me. The other is a beautiful flower painted by my dad. He came to take care of me when I broke my leg, and we would sit for hours painting together. From one perspective, or frame, breaking my leg was distressing—it forced me to slow down and endure physical pain. From another frame, it was a blessing—I enjoyed quality time with my dad, rekindled my inner painter, and went on a creative sabbatical. We have infinite ways to "frame" and thus perceive our experience.

The four sides of a frame contain a picture. If you were looking at a piece of art, the frame defines what is included on the canvas and what is not. It sets the parameters and contains the image. A gifted artist friend of mine says, "What you leave out of the frame is just as important as what you put in the frame." The frames I refer to in this chapter are not wooden or metal structures but the hidden mental constructs framing and defining our communication and experience. Living in Supreme Influence, you are aware of mental frames, and you know how to consciously create or transform them.

Let's explore what "frames" specifically are:

A frame is the boundary through which a situation is perceived. Frames contain and perpetuate a particular point of view. You continually set frames—*time frames, relationship frames, possibility* or *impossibility frames*—to serve as parameters that give context and meaning to your experience. Your map of the world is made up of frames. You perceive reality through frames whether you are aware of it or not. These frames contain many internal representations (IRs) and thus influence what you see, hear, feel, and attract in a universe of infinite possibility.

We continually set frames and move in and out of frames. Some frames shift from moment to moment; others are deeply entrenched. If someone feels stuck in a problem and can't see his way out, his focus is fixed on a particular frame. It's a case of *temporary tunnel vision*. He is unable to see outside the confines of the "problem frame." Even if a solution is available, it is not apparent to him yet. Someone may offer feedback, saying: "Think outside the box!" The wisdom in this cliché is real—creativity and innovation exist outside the frame (or box) of previous thinking.

To think outside the box, first it's important to realize there *is* a box. Often, like a fish in a fishbowl, we can be so immersed in a frame that it's a revelation to realize we are in it!

There are endless ways to frame your experience. Any situation can be observed from an infinite number of angles. Life can be perceived through limitless points of view. You have the power to shift frames at will. In this chapter you will learn how to construct empowering frames and transform limiting boundaries so *you* become *the Frame Master*—the one who knows how to consciously create and transform mental frames at will.

FRAMES SET THE STAGE
TO MANIFEST YOUR VISION

Pretend your friend went to a party and filmed it. She focused her camera on a couple in a corner who were arguing. She then showed you the film. You may say, "Yikes! That party looked awful! I'm glad I skipped it." But if your friend went to the same party and filmed people dancing to live music, smiling, laughing, nibbling on delicious foods, and relishing fun and enthusiasm, then your response would reflect a different perspective: "Wow, that party looks fantastic!" Your perception would mirror the information captured in the frame, based on where she chose to focus the lens.

You are a filmmaker. You have *choice* about where you focus the lens of your camera. You choose to include things in the frame and exclude others. You decide what is relevant or irrelevant, useful or not. You can zoom in and magnify certain things, or zoom out and let other things fade into black. You determine whose perspective will be amplified or minimized, sharpened or blurred. You are the director! With your attention and intention, you are filming the magnum opus called *My Life*.

Here are a few reasons why consciously setting frames will benefit you:

Increased Flexibility and Choice

Setting frames gives you greater choice within the context of what's most important to you. Frames that work in one context may not work in another. A CEO may have a clear "outcome frame," and thus be in a superefficient, high-velocity, get-to-the-point state of mind to achieve her outcome. She will want to switch frames before entering the bedchamber with her lover. Flexibility is power. A frame that works brilliantly in one context can yield disaster in another. Frame Masters are present to the environment. They set appropriate frames, in alignment with their purpose, for each particular context.

Clear Objectives and Focus

Setting frames allows you to set parameters in advance. A frame gives structure. It allows you to build a foundation for communication and understanding. If you give yourself a time frame of five minutes to complete a task, your energy can be focused on accomplishing that task, which streamlines your purpose and expedites achieving your goal.

Frames provide focus for how you speak and act. Have you ever sat in a business meeting and wondered, *What is the point of this meeting? How soon will it be over?* This is an indicator that the meeting facilitator did a poor job setting frames beforehand. He was not clear on the time frame and meeting objectives. When a meeting has structure with clear parameters, then it's easy to focus results within those frames: *By the end of this two-hour session today, we will have generated three potential ideas for our new brand.* Clarity is power. Frames direct attention and punctuate points. Without frames people can become lost, bored, or focused on low-priority tasks. Setting frames creates common understanding, unifying hearts and minds toward a shared vision.

Creating Agreement

Frames create a context for mutual agreement. In my courses I intentionally and immediately set frames to create a secure container for our work and to empower those present to let go of the past and step into their power. I create learning frames that support students in integrating knowledge more rapidly and practically. I establish feedback frames that guide them in learning how to give and receive the most effective feedback. I set participation frames that demonstrate how to have fun and maximize our time. These frames, and others, cocoon the student and create a sacred space for conscious transformation.

Efficiency

Frames limit choice by determining which information will be included or excluded. This saves you valuable time, because your brain doesn't get bogged down or distracted by analyzing too much sensory data. For example, if you hold the frame that you are a raw-foods vegan and you go grocery shopping in a chain-store supermarket, you wouldn't need to walk through all the aisles. You would stride directly to the fruits and vegetables section and efficiently make your selections.

SET OUTCOME FRAMES TO ACHIEVE SUCCESSFUL RESULTS

Anytime I schedule a meeting, I ask myself, *What is the ultimate outcome for this meeting? What result am I inspired to produce?*

How specifically will I know when it has been achieved? What will I see, hear, and feel when it is accomplished? These questions support me in establishing an "outcome frame."

You always achieve an outcome. An outcome is a result; a result is unavoidable. It may be your desired result—*or not.* Either way, your communication and actions produce outcomes. The reason to set an outcome frame in advance is to create the prime conditions for success. Outcome frames support you in being laser focused on what you are dedicated to accomplish. The key is to zero in on your outcome while simultaneously expanding your awareness. This ensures the magic of the moment is revealed.

Anytime you wish to consciously create something, choose what you want. Without clear objectives you lose direction, like a ship without a heading. When you have one specific, clear objective, you can move *full speed ahead.* Remember step two of the Ten-Step Formula for Conscious Creation in chapter 12: *Choose what you intend to create or experience.*

People will continually project their frames on to you, whether you recognize those frames or not. If someone else has a clear objective and you do not, it's possible to get sucked into his outcome frame, often without realizing it. That frame may or may not be in alignment with your purpose. When you have a clear outcome frame, you won't get distracted. You concentrate on priorities.

Be clear with your objective. Act with single-minded focus. Listen for Supreme guidance. Trust your intuition. Allow the Universe to grant you the fruits of your actions without feeling the need to control how it shows up.

You can set outcome frames for any activity. If you were to go out to dinner with a friend, you could have a richer experience by declaring an intention: *I intend to create the vibe where my friend feels totally loved, appreciated, and supported.* This declaration could create a richer, more meaningful experience than just getting together to "hang out."

If someone grumbles about "what's wrong" or "what's *not* happening" in that moment, she is unclear about her desired outcome—unless her objective is to complain, which is doubtful. When people speak of what they don't want, they are perceiving a situation through a "problem frame." You can hear it in their language. They ask questions and make statements that assume problems.

We live at a perpetual crossroads. We have freedom to choose and power to create. From moment to moment, we are either aware of our choices, and thus choosing wisely, or we are unaware, and thus choosing ignorantly. The choices we make yield corresponding consequences. Making a simple switch from a problem frame to an outcome frame changes one's direction and trajectory.

Consider the examples below. Notice how language shapes and reveals the frame someone holds:

PROBLEM FRAME	OUTCOME FRAME
What's wrong?	What am I inspired to accomplish?
Why is this happening?	How can I create or attract what I want?
What/who caused this problem?	What resources are available?
I don't want ____ to happen.	I choose to create ____.
I don't want to worry about ____.	I'm committed to materialize ____.

If someone is in a problem frame, you can pose a purposeful question to help him shift his focus: "I recognize you don't want _____. What do you want instead?" Be present and listen intently to his response. Your question can successfully support the person in stepping outside the boundaries of the old problem frame and into a frame of possibility.

The actions you take match the frames you hold. When you set an outcome frame, you program your RAS. At lightning speed your mind and senses sort through limitless data, deleting, distorting, generalizing, and attracting information that fits in the boundaries of your frames.

Life hands you frames with limited information—whole chunks will be deleted, distorted, and generalized. It's up to you to direct your mind and focus on the bits that elevate your life. Use the meta-model to discover deletions and distortions in communication, which in turn allow you to more clearly understand another's map of reality.

FRAME SIZE

When you set frames, you set parameters. How wide is the lens? How broad is your perspective? The size of the frame changes your perception. This is one reason why it is unwise to judge anyone or anything at first glance. When you look at something or someone, you initially see only a tiny fraction of the whole.

Suppose a camera filmed a close-up of a man with leathery skin, a mustache over tightly closed lips, and a furrowed brow. You wonder who he is and why he looks so intense. As the camera begins to pull back, you notice that he wears a cowboy hat, a bandanna around his neck, a leather vest, and a gun holster and he carries a rifle. You see another man on his right, in a similar getup and stance, holding a bottle of Jack Daniels. The camera pulls out farther and you see a stoic-faced woman on his left. She wears a big hat with feathers and elbow-high satin gloves, and she's also holding a gun. As the frame widens, you see a little girl holding a rifle sitting next to the woman. Now the camera frame is so wide you see a photographer with an antique camera saying, "Cheese." You realize this is a family having a Wild West portrait taken at the county fair. All around are spectators laughing and enjoying a spectacular, sunny day.

The parameters—or size—of the frame change *everything*. Look beyond borders. Observe, contemplate, and ask questions. Life is continually presenting us with pieces to a bigger puzzle.

Things that appear true at one level of consciousness may be incomplete teachings when viewed from expanded realms of understanding. I've studied ancient wisdom texts for more than eighteen years. As my consciousness expanded, so did my understanding. Over the years certain passages have come alive with deeper, richer, more expansive meanings than I initially interpreted. As the frame of my awareness grew, so did my comprehension.

There is a parable known as the Blind Men and the Elephant that originated in ancient India. It illustrates how people perceive different truths based on frame size. A group of blind men touch an elephant. Each man touches only one part of the animal. The man who touches the trunk says, "The elephant is like a tree trunk." The man touching the tusk says, "The elephant is like a solid pipe." The man touching the tail says, "The elephant is like a rope." The man who touches the leg says, "The elephant is like a pillar." Though they described the same animal, each man had his own point of view that was limited in perspective. Without honoring one another's perspective, and without the will and skill to intelligently communicate, misunderstandings about what is "real" could escalate and cause conflict—each man believing he is right and the other wrong, when in actuality each is experiencing just one dimension of a bigger truth.

HAKALAU: TRANSCEND TUNNEL VISION WITH EXPANDED AWARENESS

The ability to widen frame size can be learned. In Hawaiian Shamanism there is the term *Hakalau*, which is a form of walking meditation that Kahunas practice to access a neutral, relaxed state of expanded awareness.

This practice allows you to focus on the result you are committed to *while* simultaneously being aware of the infinite possibilities surrounding you. You want to zero in on your outcome, see it in your mind's eye, and *at the same time* be fully expanded in peripheral vision. This practice activates and heightens your senses.

In NLP, it is considered the "Learning State," and it is believed to increase cognition and the ability to learn. Hakalau is the safest way to drive your car and navigate your body temple.

The test of a first-rate intelligence
is the ability to hold two opposed ideas
in the mind at the same time, and
still retain the ability to function.
—F. SCOTT FITZGERALD

PREFRAMES STIMULATE RAS
TO NOTICE WHAT YOU WANT

When you are in a state of expanded awareness, you recognize a multitude of frames. You can consciously choose the most befitting frame for a given situation. From a broader perspective, you can purposefully narrow your focus to achieve a specific result.

One masterful way of using frames is a linguistic tool called preframing. Preframing is consciously setting a frame in advance and speaking it into existence. A properly delivered preframe guides attention. This allows you and others to perceive through the frame you created.

Let's go back to the story about the friend who is filming a couple arguing at a party. Suppose your friend *preframed* you, informing you that her intent was to film footage for a documentary titled *Understanding Emotions in Intimate Relationships*. She was specifically seeking scenes of couples displaying emotion. Instead of perceiving the party through the frame of "Yikes! The party looked awful," you would congratulate her. The frame through which you look alters your perspective.

When you set a frame in advance, you stimulate the RAS to magnify certain things and bypass others. You create parameters—then the brain goes to work looking for details that fit within that frame. Looking for a frame causes it to manifest. Like the results of the observer effect, the process of observation has creative power.

Allow me to illustrate another preframe. If I said to you:

> *Time is a mental construct, which means that how each*
> *one of us experiences time is different. Can you remember*
> *a situation when time moved sooooo slooooww? (Like when*

you are waiting in a long line?) How about a time when
time moved very quickly? (Like when you are having fun
with someone you love?) What if you had a tool, a practice
that supported you in stretching or condensing time? What
would that be worth? How inspired would you be if you had
one additional hour per day to focus on anything you want?
In a moment, I'm going to share with you some profound
insights on how you can masterfully frame time.

By delivering the preframe above, I've properly served up what is to come, and you'd be excited to hear what I have to say. In contrast, if I just walked into a room and started sharing a meditation exercise without offering a preframe, you might feel lost or unmotivated to listen.

A properly delivered preframe sets the stage. It gets people on the edge of their seats waiting for what you will say next. When you deliver a presentation, it is wise to preframe: let your audience know—up front—what they can expect to walk away with. If you examine the introduction to this chapter and others, you'll see that I preframe your experience by illuminating what you will be learning and why it's valuable.

Here's an empowering frame you can look through: *you are a divine being with limitless potential; you have the power to shift frames at will.*

CONSCIOUS EVOLUTION AND UPDATING FRAMES

Often we perceive through frames without thinking about what's happening. Sometimes people aren't aware of the frame they hold. To them, it's a belief that is true in their reality. Some frames serve you; others may be up for review. As you become more aware of frames, you keep the ones that work for you and transform those that don't. Be aware. Ask yourself, *Are the frames I am looking through supporting my magnificence?*

There are limitless frames and combinations of frames. Challenges arise when parameters of a frame become too constricted and no longer serve the highest good. Many decades ago, a frame existed in the business world that asserted men should be paid more than women. As more women penetrated the workforce, this frame was challenged and replaced by a new one: *equal pay for equal work*. Frames around gender roles have been shifting throughout the past few generations. Frames are not static. We can create new worlds by creating new frames.

We each hold individual frames developed from our life experience. Collectively, we also hold culturally agreed-upon frames. Rules, laws, and taboos are frames that define what is considered acceptable or unacceptable, moral or immoral, possible or not possible. These frameworks allow us to share a common experience of reality. We may not all share the same frames, but we are collectively affected by the consequences of *cultural* frames. Around the world, a red light means "stop." When we roll up to a red light, we choose to stop. This is a shared frame in which our actions align. A correlating frame warns us, "If you don't stop at a red light, you get a ticket." Setting frames that people can agree on allows interactions (and traffic!) to flow.

VALUES FRAMES

Some of our most powerful individual frames are "values" frames. We each have a set of values that characterize what we believe and deem important.

Values frames allow you to form a particular, chosen life experience. Frames can direct you to choose wisely. They provide a shortcut to decision making. When you set your frame in advance, it can be relied on to filter information. If you hold the frame that you value the environment, you remember to bring your reusable grocery bag every time you shop. That action does not require thought. It fits within your frame, and your behavior consistently flows from the frame. If you didn't hold that frame, you'd probably expect to receive plastic or paper bags each time you shopped, and you'd discard the bags after one use without a thought. Often, options outside your boundaries don't appear on your radar unless someone specifically points them out. Frames support lifestyle decisions—your choices are filtered through your frames.

One summer afternoon, while on vacation with my parents off the coast of Florida, I had an experience that imprinted my psyche with an empowering frame I've held my entire life. I was 3 years old, and we were at the hotel pool. My dad jumped in the water, while my mom sat on a beach chair catching the sun's rays. Walking around the pool's perimeter, I noticed something I had never seen before: a diving board. Cautiously I climbed on the board, walked to the edge, and looked over. The water seemed infinitely farther than it actually was. My dad saw me on the edge and shouted, "Jump!" My mom turned her head, saw us both, and screamed, "Don't jump!" Then she yelled at my dad, "Valentine! . . . Don't you dare have her jump!" My dad paid no attention and urged me on. My mom persisted, "Stop! Don't jump!" I was in a bind—a bit of a crisis for a 3-year-old. I had to make a decision. Do I listen to Mom or Dad? Then my dad said, "If you jump, I'll take you to Disney World!" I got excited and jumped! The intensity of that moment, and the result of my decision, carved a profound imprint in my psyche: *When I take risks and jump in, even if it's scary, I am safe and rewarded.* From that moment on, I've viewed life through that frame. I don't hesitate to take risks for what's important to me. Deeply imprinted experiences from childhood often form the frames through which we perceive and create reality. In this example my dad was present and careful when he urged me to jump. If another child in a similar scenario jumped and broke a bone, then she would likely perceive life through a very different frame.

TIME FRAMES

Here's another fun story of an event from my childhood that influenced how I frame and ultimately perceive and navigate the concept of *time*.

I vividly remember the time my cousin came from Cuba. I was 8, and she was one year younger. She had never owned a doll. My dad took us to the toy store and said we had *five minutes* to get whatever we wanted, as much as we could fit into one cart. It was an exhilarating day that left a profound imprint in my consciousness—*I could have whatever I want as long as I am smart with my time.*

Einstein proved time is relative. You can play with the boundaries of time—stretching or condensing it in your mind to match your vision. How you frame time influences your experience and decisions.

Most of us have experienced a challenging or traumatizing experience that at the moment seemed like the most horrific event on the planet. Years or even decades later, you realize you would never be where you are today, or the person you have become, if not for that experience. You find yourself feeling immense gratitude for the experience, and you know that if given the chance, you wouldn't change a thing. Or maybe you've faced an embarrassing moment, and at that instant you wanted to evaporate or just disappear, only to have a friend say, "One day you'll look back on this and laugh." But it didn't seem funny *in the moment*. What if *one day* was today? What if you could use the framing power of your mind to float above time and see the event unfold below you? How then would the perception and feeling transform?

If you felt stuck in a problem, you could direct your consciousness out toward the future. Imagine mentally traveling beyond the successful resolution of your problem to a place where you experience new resources and insights. Time is a construct you can navigate in your mind to gain a broader perspective that enables wiser decisions.

Time is the moving image of eternity.

−PLATO

Have you ever procrastinated until an impending deadline loomed over you, demanding immediate action? As you approached the zero hour, did you find yourself accomplishing tasks with superhuman velocity? We communicate and respond differently based on time frames.

It makes sense to view time differently when you create a

yearly sales and marketing plan than when you enjoy an intimate evening. If your are structuring a sales and marketing plan, you want to step outside of the moment and look at a timeline, like a ruler in front of you, where you can analyze the past and project into the future. With this perspective you learn from past mistakes and generate new forecasts. However, using this time frame when you make love would be a drag! A more appropriate frame for an intimate encounter would be surrendering into the eternal now, dissolving into the beloved, and losing your mind to pleasure.

Mystics speak of extracting the nectar of life. The Sufi mystics, as well as the sages of ancient India, teach a profound meditation that initiates consciousness into expanded realms of understanding. It is known as *die while you are alive*. In this ritual you experience your own death in advance by floating to the future. First you arrive at a time when you are very old and in good health. Then you appear at the moment of your death. Great wisdom comes as you commune with the older sagacious you, and you come to know your *self* more completely. Therefore, let us die while we are alive, that we may come to know our immortality and live each day as though it is our last and, in this frame, give from the depth of our beautiful heart and sacred soul.

Almost everything—all external expectations, all pride, all fear of embarrassment or failure—these things just fall away in the face of death, leaving only what is truly important. Remembering that you are going to die is the best way I know to

avoid the trap of thinking you have something to
lose. You are already naked. There is no reason
not to follow your heart.

–STEVE JOBS

VISIONARIES CREATE FRAMES

Visionaries create frames rather than mindlessly buying into old ones or copying someone else's. Walt Disney set out to create the "Happiest Place on Earth," and his decisions were filtered through that frame. Having grown up in Miami, I remember how profoundly the Disney brand imprinted my childhood. If you visit Disneyland or Disney World, you become immersed in their frame. Disney uses language to perpetuate their frame. Disney doesn't have "employees"; they have "cast members." The cast members don't wear "uniforms"; they wear "costumes." These presuppositions sustain the frame that Disney creates a theatrical world of magic.

The most successful companies and brands have strong and clearly communicated frames. They set parameters that employees and consumers buy into. Steve Jobs's Apple Inc. is an example of a company with powerful frames. The Apple frame is embodied in the 1984 slogan "Think Different." When consumers purchase an Apple product, they're not just buying a piece of machinery. They are buying into a frame and aligning themselves with Apple's counterculture and artistic ethos. Apple doesn't sell MP3 players, computers, and smartphones—it sells a lifestyle. And innovation, simplicity, and elegance go inside that frame. Mercedes-Benz doesn't sell cars; it sells luxury and sophistication. Victoria's Secret doesn't sell underwear; it sells sex and femininity. Strong brands have clear frames.

When people do not share a frame, they work independently and sometimes at cross-purposes. Right after initiating a professional relationship, I was sitting with the head honcho of a highly successful automotive dealership. His office overlooked the showroom floor. Several prospective customers walked on the lot, but no salesperson or manager was in sight. Controlling his anger, the leader picked up his phone and, with poise, paged, "Mr. *New*-man, you have a guest on the showroom floor. Mr. *New*-man." This was a code the salespeople knew well. It meant *get to the showroom immediately and service Mr. "new" man.*

I asked if there were enough people scheduled for the shift. He replied yes. I asked, "Who's the shift manager?" He said, "Phil." "Where is he?" I asked. He snapped, "I don't know, but he should be on the sales floor right now!" I continued: "What specifically is most important in Phil's job description? What is his number-one responsibility?" The leader replied, "To make sure every customer experiences world-class service so we sell more cars." "I'll go talk to Phil," I said.

When I found Phil, he was in his office, on the phone, with his door closed. When he got off the phone, I asked, "Phil, what is the most important responsibility you have as a manager here?" Phil's response: "To recruit top salespeople." Phil was in his office behaving in alignment with his frame. Phil "not being on the showroom floor" was not the *problem*. It was a symptom of a bigger problem—team members not being on the same page. Thus, people were reacting based on their frames, which may or may not (in this case not!) have been in alignment with the company's frames. I worked with the executives and team members throughout all departments, enrolling everyone in the process of creating clear, shared frames. Their results skyrocketed!

Decisions are filtered through frames. When everyone on a team shares the same core values, the company's power becomes focused in a unified direction, which yields success.

Leaders understand the value of establishing and communicating frames. They focus on the big picture—not details. A paradigm-shattering example is Martin Luther King Jr. In the United States during the early civil rights movement, a cultural frame posited that black people and minorities were inferior and white people were somehow superior. This propagated a perception that people should be segregated and treated differently according to race. Because this frame existed in the larger culture, many decisions, actions, and laws supported this frame. Black people were bused to different schools and not allowed to attend certain colleges and universities; they had to sit at the back of the bus and surrender their seats to a white person. Awake beings, including Martin Luther King Jr., did not buy into this frame. Dr. King articulated a different frame: *All men are created equal.* He was on purpose; he held this frame congruently. Eventually, his frame shattered the old one. He didn't waste time trying to change parts of the whole—the laws and policies of the bus company, school system, government agencies, and churches. He recognized that the way to shift these infractions was to shatter the prevailing frame and introduce a new frame big enough to honor all beings. Decisions and actions are filtered through frames. When the overarching frame changes, everything transforms.

Whoever is most congruent is the person who sets the frame.

Others will be persuaded to accept the frame to the degree it is clearly and congruently communicated.

REFRAMING: SHIFT CONTEXT/MEANING TO TRANSFORM EXPERIENCE

Martin Luther King Jr. changed the cultural frame. He and other civil rights activists successfully dismantled an old frame and replaced it with one honoring life and empowering all people. This is an example of a reframe. Reframing is a process that swaps out old frames for new frames. It transforms the frame through which one perceives. Reframing causes you to step outside the boundaries of a problem and see it in a new light—that is, a new frame.

If a person feels "stuck," he is anchored in a frame, viewing things from a certain perspective within particular parameters. Reframing can be a profoundly gentle way of transforming thinking. It lifts veils, allowing the person to sidestep into a new reality. It's also a mighty tool to explore your own mind.

Here's an example of a reframe. My transformational live courses are designed with moments that evoke confusion. Confusion is a signal that you are stretching beyond old paradigms. Confusion often precedes a breakthrough. However, some people are uncomfortable experiencing confusion, because it triggers old memories or deep programming like "I'm slow," "I'm never going to get it," "I'll be left behind," or "I'm stupid." If someone says, "I'm confused," I offer a reassuring smile. Then I say, "Fantastic! If you weren't confused, you probably wouldn't be learning much because you would already know what I am saying. Confusion means your consciousness is expanding. Your brain is searching for answers. Being confused is evidence that learning is indeed happening and that you are elevating into an understanding previously outside your awareness. That's great news!"

Let's look at confusion from a linguistic perspective. If you divide the word *confusion* into its roots, you have the base words *con* and *fusion*. *Con* means "with" and *fusion* means "merging," or "melting together." So *confusion* means new associations are being formed. That's how learning happens. With this example, I reframe the meaning of *confusion* by taking something seemingly negative and transforming it into something valuable.

I once heard Richard Bandler, the genius who cocreated NLP, reframe confusion:

> In our workshops, we're always telling you success is the
> most dangerous human experience, because it keeps you
> from noticing other things and learning other ways of
> doing things. That also means any time you fail, there's an
> unprecedented opportunity for you to learn something you
> wouldn't otherwise notice. Confusion is the doorway to
> reorganizing your perceptions and learning something new.
> If you were never confused, that would mean everything
> that happened to you fit your expectations, your model
> of the world, perfectly. Life would simply be one boring,
> repetitive experience after another.

Now that we have an idea of what a reframe is, let's explore a few different ways to wield this linguistic tool. Two examples of reframes are *meaning reframe* and *context reframe*.

The meaning reframe is a language pattern with the potency to change the meaning of an existing behavior or experience. The example of confusion is a meaning reframe. It elevated and redefined the meaning of "confusion." You can employ this technique by taking a behavior or situation considered negative and directing the RAS to notice a different set of attributes. You thus see the behavior or situation from a different angle, which changes the meaning.

The context reframe premises the idea that *every* behavior can be useful in some context. Finding an appropriate context for a behavior shifts the frame. Would your behavior at a formal dinner party be the same as at a Super Bowl party? Perhaps not! Context influences how you choose to perceive a situation and how you act within it.

Celine Dion, the world-renowned singer, delivered a brilliant context reframe during an interview when she was asked about her husband René's "gambling problem." Here was Dion's response: "René's a gambler. Of course he is. And I'm glad he is . . . because he mortgaged his house to make me do my first album when I was 12 years old. That's probably the biggest gamble he's ever done." Dion took something that could be perceived as a problem—her husband's gambling—and reframed it into a positive benefit simply by switching the context.

REFRAMING FAILURE

NLP declares: *There is no failure, only feedback*. This statement gives you a reframe of "failure." Rather than viewing unfulfilled desires as "failures," see them as valuable feedback you wouldn't have seen otherwise. Some of my greatest lessons have come in contrast to a seeming setback. Napoleon Hill said, "Every adversity . . . carries with it the seed of an equal or greater benefit." Let's mine our challenges for the jewels inside. Anytime a situation arises you want to change, observe it in the *feedback frame: This is feedback about what isn't working. What can I learn from this, the learning of which will elevate everything? What do I want instead? What opportunity can be mined from this challenge?*

If someone views a situation from the frame of "failure," it's more likely she will give up too soon. If someone views a situation through the frame of "feedback," she can be infinitely flexible and change her approach until she accomplishes her goal.

I intentionally set up the feedback frame in my courses. If someone practices an exercise and has trouble grasping the concept, I encourage her to continue practicing while noticing what works and what could be improved.

REFRAME QUESTIONS

Reframing is a powerful tool for composing new meaning for something that challenges you (or someone else). If you ever feel stuck in a moment and can't seem to navigate out of a problem frame—an old habit creeps up or a disempowering story loops—use a reframe to dismantle the old frame and offer fresh perspective.

The following questions have power to reframe because they cannot be answered in the problem frame. In other words, you (or the other person) *must* look outside the boundaries of the problem frame to answer them. The last few questions can even blow the boundaries off old frames altogether! Anytime you find yourself in a predicament, play with these questions.

Contemplate them. If you are using them to reframe another person's perspective, give the recipient the space to search for an answer. Unlike the process of asking *empowering questions* (taught in the previous chapter), when you ask reframe questions, instruct your mind to search for specific answers. They will come, and you will see with new eyes.

REFRAME QUESTIONS

What can I learn from this?

What else could this mean?

What's funny about this? (If your brain says *Nothing!* then ask . . .)

If there were something funny, what would it be?

What is the gift here?

In what context would this behavior be useful or appropriate?

What would happen if I didn't have this problem?

What wouldn't happen if I didn't have this problem?

What have I been pretending not to know to have thought I had that problem?

What would happen if I did create what I really want?

This is a conscious inquiry. Take your time and thoroughly ask and answer each question. Enjoy the process, and you will discover new dimensions of thinking and being.

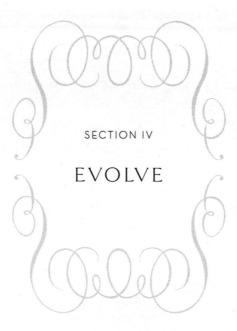

SECTION IV

EVOLVE

16

YOUR INFINITE POINT OF VIEW

Now you understand what *frames* are, and you realize there are endless ways to frame your experience. Any situation can be observed from an infinite number of angles. Life can be perceived through limitless points of view. You have the power to shift frames at will. This chapter guides you in navigating multiple perceptual positions so you can easily view things from different perspectives. This expanded awareness enriches your map of reality by offering amplified choices and enabling you to make wiser decisions.

A *perceptual position* is the point of awareness from which you experience reality. You can see the world through your own perspective or through someone else's. You can become the neutral observer or take the perspective of an older, wiser version of self. Through your imagination, you have the power to perceive life through infinite perceptual positions.

We've all heard the adage: *Step into another man's shoes, and see from his perspective.* When you step into another's shoes, you experience a different perceptual position than what you see through your own eyes. When you explore different perceptual positions, you gain resources from a universal awareness that is unavailable simply by seeing through your own physical eyes.

Each perceptual position is a frame. It offers parameters

or boundaries through which you perceive the moment. Here are four major perceptual positions you can navigate to gain insightful perspectives and amplified choice.

- *First position: fully associated*—"I"
  You see through your own eyes, hear through your own ears, and feel your own feelings. Anytime you are emotionally involved, you are fully associated in first position. If someone feels stuck in a problem, and they can't *see their way out,* they are anchored in first position. Pursuing your own dreams, setting boundaries, and caring for yourself are manifestations of first-position association. Here you make decisions based on what makes sense from your immediate point of view.
- *Second position: dissociated*—"You"
  You see through someone else's eyes. You enter the other person's map of the world. Second position is the "other." You see through others' eyes, hear with *their* ears, and feel with *their* feelings. You believe *their* beliefs, and value what *they* value. You sense *their* desires. Second position is useful anytime you encounter resistance. It helps you experience compassion, build rapport, and understand another's map. It is invaluable in modeling excellence within a particular context. You can pick a model of possibility, someone who is a master at something you choose to learn; then, see, hear, and feel from that person's perspective so that you integrate new tools and resources.
- *Third position: dissociated*—"Observer"
  Neutrally observe the experience, from high above or faraway or as though the action occurs on a movie screen. Third position, the "observer," is useful when encountering obstacles. When emotions run high, third position is an

excellent way of calming, gaining perspective, and recognizing new resources. No negative emotions exist in third position, because you are in a point of awareness that is neutral and unidentified. You see, hear, and feel from the position of a detached observer and thus gain an overview or "big picture" of situations. You can analyze logically, without emotional involvement. You can heal past wounds by observing them and gathering insights and learning. Here you see yourself as others see you.

- *Supreme superposition: compassionate dissociation—"We"*
  This is a multidimensional superposition, meaning that your consciousness honors and owns your individual perspective (without attachment) while simultaneously honoring the whole of humanity and all existence. Here you see beyond duality into unity. In the *Supreme superposition*, you (1) see through your own eyes, (2) simultaneously see through the eyes of another, (3) see through the eyes of the people, and (4) observe at the same time in eternal stillness. You respect all beings as unique and indivisible aspects of one organism, whole and complete. And you recognize that what you do to another, you do to yourself. This is a superconscious position, meaning you are aware of how your energy, thoughts, words, and choices influence others and create an infinite ripple effect. And you care. Like a bodhisattva, you think, speak, and act with compassion. Embodying the Supreme superposition is the mark of a genuine leader, one who embraces cooperation. For example, Gandhi and Nelson Mandela are models of the Supreme superposition.

Play with this knowledge. If you wish to buy a pair of shoes that fit properly, you want to try them on, walk around, and see how they feel on your feet. It's the same here. You can move back and forth among perceptual positions. As you do, fully experience them. See a situation from multiple angles before making an educated choice.

Navigating these four perceptual positions provides a new way of looking at the same experience, offering you greater choice on how to respond. In Hakalau, discussed in the previous chapter, you hold first and third positions simultaneously, although you could continue to expand awareness to realize the Supreme superposition, which has the most influence because you are conscious and caring.

Positions one through three can be useful in some contexts; however, they can create challenges when applied in other contexts. If someone feels overwhelmed by a problem, it's guaranteed that he is stuck in first position with blinders on. Narcissistic behavior is a result of being trapped in the boundaries of first position. The simple act of inhaling a conscious breath and stepping outside the situation, allowing perspective to shift from first to second or third position, reveals options previously hidden. If someone gets fixed in second position, she might lose her own perspective and absorb another person's emotions, beliefs, or thoughts. If someone becomes anchored predominantly in third position, it's possible to disengage from life altogether, becoming distant and intimately unavailable. The Supreme superposition offers the greatest awareness while honoring all beings.

Your experience of reality will be directly linked to the perceptual positions you frequent. Living in Supreme Influence, you are aware of multiple perceptual positions and are free to fluidly move through them, consciously and without attachment. It's possible to be in multiple perceptual positions at once—as in Supreme superposition—because consciousness is nonlocal, meaning your mind is not encased into any one particular location. You can simultaneously see through your own eyes, experience what someone else sees, and observe the entire dynamic unfolding in totality.

I, you, he, she, we. In the garden of mystic lovers
these are not true distinctions.

—RUMI

Walt Disney used perceptual frames brilliantly in his work. Robert Dilts documented Disney's genius with perspectives in his book *Strategies of a Genius: Volume 1*. Dilts suggests Disney would look through three distinct perceptual frames in his creative process to manifest brilliant ideas. First Disney would gaze through the frame of the "dreamer," allowing his imagination free rein to follow inspirited wild whims. Then he would look through the frame of the "realist" to determine the practical and doable. Not everything fantastical would make sense in the material world. Finally he would pass his ideas through the frame of "critic," which gave him a devil's advocate perspective of what could possibly go wrong. This way he could resolve potential challenges before they happened. These three frames were instrumental in Disney's success. They balanced one another. One without the other would not have yielded the same Magic Kingdom.

Not all those who wander are lost.

—J.R.R. TOLKIEN

17

THE ART AND SCIENCE
OF RAPPORT

Imagine having the ability to instantly create a deep, authentic connection with anyone anytime. You do. This is the power of rapport.

Everything you could want to accomplish or create in your life requires rapport. Rapport opens the door to every relationship. It's essential for success. Powerfully bringing your gifts to the world requires building cooperative relationships created through rapport.

Rapport is a relationship of responsiveness. When you are in rapport with someone, you relate in harmony. You are open to each other's suggestions; the energy is reciprocal. Rapport is a deep connection that bypasses analytical filters. Judgment or doubt is suspended and communication happens fluidly. Rapport creates a sense of closeness. With rapport, you open the door to relating, connecting, negotiating, and reaching agreements in a reasonable way. The purpose of this chapter is to reveal the real nature and power of rapport and to show you how to authentically cultivate it.

THE PROCESS OF RAPPORT

The first time I heard the word *rapport*, I was 15. It was my first day of selling knives door-to-door. My manager said, "People buy from people they like and trust. You must build rapport right away." I thought this was a bizarre mandate, since I intuited that cultivating "like" and "trust" was a natural phenomenon. Over the years, my understanding of and appreciation for the massive power of rapport evolved.

Today I know that rapport can unfold naturally, because we are all intrinsically connected. It can also be strategically created. The discipline of NLP has studied the science of rapport and turned it into a duplicable process. Anyone can learn the specific skills to build rapport.

The cliché approach for creating rapport is finding things in common: *What do you do for work? Where do you live? What do you do for fun?* A more subtle approach is *mirroring and matching*. This is where you notice subtle details of someone's state and communication and you align with them. You observe someone's rate of breathing, subtle movements, and mannerisms and you gently mirror and match her pace, tones, and rhythms. The person may not be aware that you are matching her, but she will feel a strong affinity. People like people who are like themselves. As you match someone's breathing and physiology, you can easily enter her map of the world and experience life from her perspective.

Following is a fun mirroring and matching exercise that you can do with a friend to more deeply understand his map of the world.

Entering Another's Map

Pick a partner and preframe him for this activity. Ask your partner to recall a vivid, *empowering* experience, a memory like a graduation, the birth of a baby, a wedding, or something similar having a rich internal representation. Instruct your partner to sit still, close his eyes, and access the memory (make sure it's an *empowering* memory) as though the experience is happening right now. Ask him to see through his own eyes, hear what he heard in that moment, and feel the feelings as though it is happening now. Have him breathe the way he was breathing. In short, guide him to notice every detail of that experience, in his mind's eye, as though he is reliving it *now*.

Then *you*, without knowing the content of your partner's experience, will begin to mirror and match his subtle movements. Match his breathing, posture, facial expression, and any other relevant detail. When *you* precisely mirror and match, *you* will soon get an impression—sometimes an instant knowing, like a download or a picture or feeling, of your partner's experience. Trust your intuition.

I've done this exercise with groups. Often I'll pair people with someone they've never met. Once, a woman in my class sat silently recalling the birth of her first son, and when her partner mirrored and matched, he soon blurted out, "Oh my gosh! I'm having a baby!" Another woman was able to feel her partner surfing a wave with the water misting her face. Consistently, more than half of the class was able to tap into his or her partner's experience. This exercise demonstrates that at the level of thought, we are all connected.

WITH GREAT POWER COMES
GREAT RESPONSIBILITY

With rapport, you can easily influence someone to your way of thinking. This is why integrity is of utmost importance. Here's a short story about choosing with your head and heart aligned.

When I was 18, in the days before the Internet, I took a job selling dating services. I naturally connected with people, and in my first month I earned over $8,000, which felt like a lot—it was the biggest paycheck I had received at the time. One day an elderly woman came in. She had been widowed for many years and had decided she was finally ready to be in a relationship. She was nervous about meeting new people, as it had been several decades since her last date. To her credit, her desire to find a life partner overshadowed her nervousness. I sincerely wanted to help her find a life partner, but I realized immediately we had no potential matches in our database. While she sat in my office, I spoke to my manager and asked his advice. He barked, "I don't care who we have in our database, you go sell that woman our services!" I walked back to my office and gently explained to the woman we had no matches for her in our system. I wished her luck and walked her out. Then I quit my job and walked out with my head and heart aligned and my honor intact.

NAMASTE IS NATURAL RAPPORT

Living in Supreme Influence, you naturally sync in rhythm with others *and* you uplift the vibe. You don't *need* special techniques to be in rapport. You harmonize because you rec-ognize . . . *we are one.*

Real rapport is spirit meeting spirit. It's seeing the Supreme in every encounter, like a mirror reflecting yourself back to you. It's recognizing that we are all individual cells in a unified organism, like a drop of water is to the ocean. The Sanskrit greeting *namaste* means "The divine in me sees, recognizes, and honors the divine in you." With that in mind, in this moment, I say to *you*, "Namaste, Beloved. I honor you, and I am grateful we are on this journey together."

When you are in deep rapport with another, your minds and your bodies attune. You can align with someone and begin harmonizing before meeting in person. You can meet in the realm of consciousness, before coming face-to-face or speaking on the phone. This is similar to launching a prayer. Personally, I enjoy incorporating my imagination and powers of visualization into my affirmative prayers. Before I meet someone, in my mind my spirit graciously offers the other person's spirit a white rose or some other sweet gift. Then I introduce myself and state my purpose for connecting, and I let them know I will be physically calling or coming. This introduction and offering is made via energetic intent and with great love and reverence. After practicing this ritual, I consistently find that by the time we meet in person we are naturally in sync. This practice creates fertile soil for authentic, open connections to flourish.

Before creating rapport with another, it is important to be in rapport within your own being. Allow me to explain.

RAPPORT, INWARD FLUENCY, AND MOTIVATION

Milton Erickson, the father of modern hypnotherapy, said that a client (in therapy) is a client because he or she is out of rapport with his or her own subconscious mind. In other words, conscious desires and subconscious beliefs are in conflict. Creating inner rapport begins with honoring all aspects of you. If you experience conflicting thoughts or emotions, it's okay. Love yourself through it. Rather than resisting the conflict, just be present to *what is*, without judgment. Remember, even Gandhi openly admitted to feelings of anger. In your authenticity you create an opening for answers to be revealed.

Humans are multidimensional beings, and at times our desires can seem to clash. We may simultaneously want one thing, then another, creating incongruence. If the battery of one's being—*life force energy*—is powering a vehicle headed in two directions at the same time, the result will be inertia. Sometimes this occurs because people are confused, or not certain about what they want, or because they don't yet believe they deserve or can have what they truly desire.

If a person is in fear, her behavior pushes against what she doesn't want. Humans are instinctually motivated to move away from pain and toward pleasure. It's a survival mechanism biologically wired into the nervous system; all animals have it. The difference between humans and animals is that humans get to choose the meaning we assign to our experiences. Gandhi assigned an empowering meaning to fasting. He viewed the practice as an ally to help him realize his purpose. Someone with a different focus might link fasting to pain. Since the instinct to move away from pain and toward pleasure is mighty, we must consciously direct our inner compass to link immense pleasure to those behaviors matching our purpose.

What motivates you? What energizes you so profoundly that you can't wait to take action? What comes naturally for you because it's an extension of who you are? You love it, and when you're engaged in it, you slip into timelessness. Action flows, and there is no doubt; you stand in certainty and inner harmony. What is one specific expression of beauty and value that reflects your inner harmony? It could be anything. It could be a relationship you've cultivated, a sport you enjoy, the way you play piano, or how you bake chocolate chip cookies.

When you are motivated to move toward what you want, action comes naturally. It doesn't mean obstacles won't arise, but you are able to handle anything coming your way. I once asked Tony Robbins, "What motivates you?" He said, "I don't need motivation. My vision is so big it pulls me in the direction I want to go." Life is in the flow, and you are in the zone, when your motivation is inspirited toward a vision.

Where there is no vision, the people perish.
—PROVERBS 29:18

When the focus is on *not experiencing* what someone doesn't want, it's not possible for that person to achieve what he or she wants! As the psychologist and teacher Dr. Wayne Dyer said, "You can never get enough of what you don't want." Therefore, one key to inner rapport is consciously directing your attention toward an inspired vision. In the absence of a vision, a person will tend to react by pushing away from experiences perceived as painful. A textbook example of this "moving away" motivation is the bride who loses weight before the wedding, only to regain it soon after the honeymoon. Why? Her intent was not to be healthy and nurture her body temple; it was not to look fat in her pictures or wedding dress.

Other examples are:

- The entrepreneur who starts her own company not because she wants to share her gifts with the world, but because she doesn't want to work for someone else.
- The serial dater who chooses relationships not because she wants to create a loving partnership, but because she doesn't want to be alone.
- The nonconformist who wears unusual clothing not because it's a creative expression of his own essence, but because he doesn't want to be like everyone else.

There's no doubt that moving-away motivation can be powerful. It can springboard you out of an undesired experience. Pain can be a powerful motivator. People have been motivated to create incredible things in this world as a result of moving away from past suffering. It's more empowering, however, to be inspired toward a grand vision. The key is to direct your focus toward where you want to go.

How do you know when your motivation is toward something *wanted* or away from something *unwanted*? When you listen carefully to language, it becomes clear from which direction the motivation is coming. Following are a few categories of language patterns that illuminate moving-away motivation. Speak each sentence aloud and notice how it feels in your body. Tune in to the energy of moving-away motivation. Does it create inner harmony or disharmony?

Language Patterns Revealing Moving-Away Motivation

A *Necessity* is when the speaker believes he or she is without choice, bound by responsibility or obligation, rather than inspiration.

Examples: *need, must, have, should*

- I *need* to lose weight.
- I *must* call my business partner.
- I *have* to finish this e-mail.
- I *should* talk to my brother.

A *Negation* is when one's attention is contradicted, rejected, denied, or opposed.

Examples: *not, can't, won't, shouldn't, don't*

- I'm *not* ever going to be like I was.
- I *can't* trust anyone.
- I *won't* ever tell a lie.
- I *shouldn't* be listening to her.
- I *don't* want to burden you.

A *Comparison* often implies that someone is looking for an external reference or approval. Inspiration comes from within and needs no external validation.

Examples: *better, worse, less, more, rather*

- I'm going to do *better* than him at this sport.
- If I do *worse* on this test than the last one, I'll flunk.
- He loves me *less* than his previous girlfriend.

- I want to look *more* attractive than the girls in the magazines.
- I'd *rather* be somewhere else.

Moving-away motivation signals resistance. Therefore, in those situations inward fluency is likely absent. Once you become aware of moving-away motivation, you can transform it by imagining what you want and choosing *moving-toward* language.

Now let's look at language that illuminates moving-toward motivation. These categories of language patterns indicate that someone's motivation is *inspired toward* a goal or vision.

Language Patterns Revealing Moving-Toward Motivation

Possibility language shows that the speaker is "at cause" and empowered to create change.

Examples: *can, will, choose*

- I *can* absolutely support you with that.
- I *will* respond immediately.
- I *choose* you.

Empowering conjugations make life-affirming links or connections between things.

Examples: *am, are, is, becoming*

- I *am* fully present with you.
- We *are* accomplishing this today.
- It *is* happening now.
- I *am becoming* even more aware.

Living in Supreme Influence, your language is neutral and/or moving toward your vision rather than moving away. In other words, you speak about what you do want, not about what you don't want.

THE ULTIMATE RAPPORT IS WITH YOU AND YOU

The ultimate rapport is with you *and* you. Real rapport engenders feelings of well-being. In this still space, you have tremendous power to manifest your intent. Here you perform your life's work, without resistance. Your words and gestures are kind; your creations are unique. You are present and give from the depth of your being. Thought is purposeful, beliefs are aligned, vision is grand, desires match, emotions vibe high, and decisions move in a clear direction. This is *inward fluency*.

When we have rapport within ourselves, we more easily create rapport with others, and we live in harmony with nature. This state of inner harmony influences our perception and choices when we arrive at life's perpetual crossroads.

THE CROSSROADS

As a child I lived next to a railroad crossing. I felt hypnotically drawn to its center. When walking to school with Ayo, my grandpa, I would ask, "Ayo, Ayo, can we please walk on the railroad? I want to stand at the crossroad." Sometimes he would indulge me. When he didn't, I would sneak over for a few moments anyway. I didn't feel like a child when I stood there. I felt timeless and eternal, with infinite choice (that is, the powers of all directions) before me.

Experience has taught me life often foreshadows what is to come. It wasn't until two decades after my walks to school with Ayo that I consciously understood the deeper significance of the crossroads and my own life's purpose of guiding people to discern and declare their direction. The crossroads is a unique place because it is in between places. It is the space of potential where choice is at hand.

When the hearts and the minds of the people know peace, the world will know peace. There is no peace in the land without peace in the hearts and minds of the people.

—DAISAKU IKEDA

Our world is evolving. It is not the same world we were born into. Structures and systems that have shaped our societies are undergoing massive change. Right now community leaders are asking essential questions: *How do we educate our children? How do we care for our health? How do we grow our food and feed our people? How do we source and create clean energy to power our lives? What is worth valuing and where do we invest our resources?* A forthcoming adjustment in our way of living is certain. To those who cling to old ways, the transition may appear as a chaotic or frightening "emergency." But to those of us who recognize change as vital to our evolution as a species, we become the uniting force bringing order to the confusion and guiding the way to emancipation.

In the past, many believed that to succeed, it was necessary to fight and struggle. It was the Darwinian concept of survival of the fittest. This concept was based on competition for scarce resources and the idea there is not enough for everyone. In the past, the driving mentality was *How can I get ahead? How can I get more, bigger, better, faster? How can I be at the top of the chain?* This way of thinking thwarts rapport between individuals and families, in businesses, in communities, and in our global relationships.

We are moving out of a worldview based on competition for scarce resources. Life is not a struggle to survive or achieve. I remember an economics class I took in high school. I still recall the language used by my teacher to define *economics*: the allocation and distribution of "scarce" resources. This didn't resonate. So I went to the library and looked it up for myself. I discovered a similar definition. "Yikes!" was all I could think.

A few years later, I was blessed to befriend Paul Zane Pilzer, a world-renowned economist who served as economic advisor in two presidential administrations. One day while Paul and I were mountain biking in the hills of Malibu, California, he shared some of the knowledge from his book *Unlimited Wealth*. He said, "We live in a world of unlimited resources because of rapidly advancing technology." Resources like energy are not scarce. It simply takes imagination, innovation, and implementation to harness the wealth of resources surrounding us. Plus love to accomplish this in an ecological and sustainable way. This conscious approach creates the space for us to be in rapport with one another, our beloved planet, and ourselves.

Be the change you wish to see in the world.
—MAHATMA GANDHI

18

THE BRIDGING OF WORLDS

In the late 1950s, the United States and the Soviet Union engaged in a "space race," each country developing rockets and satellites to orbit planet Earth, explore the cosmos, and land on the moon. The two countries had been engaged in a battle for world supremacy, and these space programs symbolized each country's effort to claim technological, defensive, and ideological superiority.

What was interesting about this race, however, was the common experience of the astronauts who ventured into space. They reported looking back at Earth from the vast emptiness of space and realizing we are one family on this planet. From a higher perspective or expanded *frame*, it became clear that our squabbles made no sense. What really mattered, these astronauts agreed, was how we treat one another and how we sustain life on Earth.

The space race, although built on competition and ideological domination, ultimately engendered a sense of respect and peace in the astronauts who pioneered the new frontier. They let go of grievances and bridged worlds. This chapter guides you to see things from a higher frame and teaches you how to consciously use language to unify. You will learn techniques to negotiate conflict, discover the authentic intent beyond behavior, create agreement, and bridge worlds.

THE DOGS BECAME GODS ON GRAPE STREET

Conscious leaders bridge worlds by focusing on the highest aim and guiding people toward a shared vision. My friend Aqeela Sherrills is one such leader. His story offers an inspiring account of how to let go of pain, consciously communicate, and bridge worlds.

Aqeela grew up in Watts, a Los Angeles neighborhood heavily steeped in gang violence. The Bloods wore red, the Crips wore blue, and Grape Street separated the two gangs. As a child Aqeela witnessed firsthand the horrors of gang warfare. He saw friends and loved ones murdered and brutalized in an endless cycle of reciprocity for violence. The motto was "an eye for an eye, and a tooth for a tooth." Rather than perpetuating the aggression, my friend made a new choice. Aqeela recognized his community was looping an old repetitive pattern, and that to transcend the battle, it would be up to him to create a new possibility and inspire a new vision.

He figured out how to gather and engage leaders of the gangs in dialogue. He looked beyond differences and spoke to the source of their commonalities. He shared with me what he shared with them:

> You're red, we're blue, and together those colors make purple. What's the line that divides us? Grape Street. And purple is the color of royalty. We call each other "Dog," but what is "dog" spelled backwards? It's god. That's who we

really are. We're gods. All of us. And it doesn't make sense
for us to go on killing each other. An eye for an eye and a
tooth for a tooth has left us all blind and toothless. Let's
claim our divinity, our power, our purpose, and let's come
together as a community to support one another.

Aqeela brokered a peace agreement in 1992, forging a historic truce between the Bloods and the Crips, suspending the decades-long cycle of violence and retaliation. He used his language to bring a community together. He now offers his expertise supporting peace negotiations globally.

After the truce, beautiful synergies arose. Soon, "peace babies" were being born from the union of couples previously forbidden to associate with each other.

EVERY BEHAVIOR HAS A POSITIVE INTENT

Aqeela knew that in order to create harmony, he must understand each gang leader's deeper motivation and highest intent. In other words, what did each one ultimately want? What was the authentic, underlying ambition fueling the feud? What was their most genuine desire? What needs were they meeting through gang affiliation? What benefit did they gain from this rivalry? People don't do things without a perceived benefit.

Aqeela intuited that their desires could be fulfilled in healthy, productive ways, paving the way for the war to end. He wholeheartedly sought to understand. Ultimately, he discovered that at the deepest level the gang members wanted honor, freedom, security, and a sense of belonging . . . just like countless other people! However, somewhere along the way, mental wiring got crossed and behaviors like "killing" became linked with values like "honor." Aqeela did not condemn; rather, he sought to connect with each soul and understand the root cause motivating their behavior. Aqeela negotiated from a space of compassion.

What if every behavior has a positive intention?

We can transform any undesired behavior by adopting new desirable ways to meet the undesired behavior's positive intention. We can inspire and influence others to transform old habits by presenting new life-affirming practices that give them what they *really* want, thereby fulfilling their authentic intent.

Aqeela's life story had poignant and painful moments. Aqeela's 19-year-old son, Terrell, was murdered at a party by a young man who didn't know him. He merely saw Terrell wearing the colors of a rival gang, mistook him for someone else, and shot him. Although few of us experience this level of trauma, we are all affected by what happens to other members of the human race. We are one people in a unified web of existence.

How can a behavior as atrocious as murder have a positive intention? How do you find the positive intent behind unacceptable behavior? And why would we want to? Allow me to answer the latter question first, because when we seek to understand, we create the conditions to evolve.

Consider Aqeela's response to his son's murder. Aqeela searched for meaning beyond his son's death. He looked past the heartbreak a parent feels after losing a child. He resolved to honor Terrell's memory by creating positive change in his community. He asked, *What would lead this young man to commit this act? What happened in his life that brought him to that point? At what point did his parents lose the connection with their child, or did they ever have a connection? How can we heal his deep wounds so his life has meaning and purpose? How can we break the cycle of pain and suffering that created this situation? How can I create something positive and empowering from my son's death? How can we educate young people to bury their grievances, give up retaliation, and embrace forgiveness and reverence for life?*

The ego seeks to divide and separate.
Spirit seeks to unify and heal.

—A COURSE IN MIRACLES

Aqeela intuitively knew that condemning a person only perpetuates cycles of abuse, trauma, violence, and distortion. When communicating with another who is anchored in a destructive pattern, it is wise to first separate the behavior from the person. In other words, the person is accepted; the behavior is unacceptable. The boy is accepted; murder is unacceptable. Seek to understand the highest intent driving another's behavior. Enter that person's map of the world. Before communicating, consider your ultimate outcome and look at the bigger picture. Ask yourself, "What is the highest choice?" See through the following frame: *this person is a child of the Universe; this behavior does not work.* As you expand your mental frame size, you cultivate compassion and illumine new ways to contribute to and evolve our emerging world.

Recognize that each person has behaviors, but who he or she is is beyond behavior. Separating behavior from the person allows you to communicate in a neutral, resourceful way, regardless of circumstance. The moment that judgment is cast, the opportunity to connect freely and genuinely is lost.

Each one of us is a unique emanation of the Supreme. When you honor each person's map of the world, even if you don't agree with it, you can communicate more effectively.

Inhale and exhale. Breathing rhythmically helps you be centered. Through equilibrium you create the conditions for a new possibility to arise. From this space of centeredness you can guide the conversation and inspire others to transform old habits into life-affirming rituals.

Perfect love casts out fear.
If fear exists, then there is not perfect love.

—A COURSE IN MIRACLES

How could certain behaviors that seem irredeemable have a positive intention? Let's take the example of revenge. If someone grows up in an environment that links revenge with honor, he could perceive life through a frame in which vengeance is considered acceptable. The subconscious mind accepts the morality you were taught as a child; this is one of its prime directives. For someone who is raised in this setting, somewhere deep in the psyche, revenge could be intertwined with a positive intent. To discover the highest intent, the question becomes "What would revenge give you? What is the reason for revenge?" Perhaps revenge would lead to a sense of justice. Then we would ask, "What would 'justice' give you? What's the highest intention of justice?" The answer may be *honor*. Again we ask: "What does honor mean to you? What does it give you?" Honor could provide a sense of self-respect. How is self-respect a benefit? Self-respect leads to freedom. What's the highest intent of freedom? "Security" could be the response. The question would follow, "What does security give you?" Perhaps the response is "freedom" or "peace." The answers of security/freedom/peace will soon loop. In this hypothetical example, the highest intent of revenge—that is, the intent fueling the behavior—might *ultimately* be security, freedom, and/or peace. We can all relate to a desire for security and freedom, even if the behavior seems far removed. Since we can understand the desire for security and freedom, from this frame we can negotiate. We can acknowledge the positive intention, separate the behavior from the person, and discover empowering ways to fulfill the person's deepest, most authentic desires.

Aqeela separated the behavior of "murder" from the boy who "murdered" his son. He recognized the boy was acting in accordance with a distorted worldview he had inherited. The cycle of violence would not end by retaliating. The way to transcend the cycle was to heal the root of the trauma, offer possibilities, and develop a new worldview for their culture. Aqeela sought life-affirming ways to heal the wounds of his people and instill a reverence for life. He offered alternatives to gangs by creating an art sanctuary in Watts. He established a cultural center and initiated several peace interventions, creating a reverence movement. Aqeela's words were the catalyst for change:

> *Reverence is the quality of attention we give to someone or something. It's our ability to see people beyond the experiences they have had and hold space for their highest possibilities to emerge. I believe where the wounds are, the gift lies. By exposing the wounds of our personal tragedies, guilt,*

and shames, we subconsciously give permission to others to
do the same, in some cases releasing generations of pent-up
anger and aggression.

Often the area that challenges us the most is where the greatest gift resides for our evolution. A gift, which once integrated, transforms how we experience the past and opens the gates for us to create a new reality. There is a gift nestled beneath every challenge waiting to be mined for hidden treasure. Living in Supreme Influence, you gather the learning and let go of grievances.

The wound is the place where
the light enters you.

—RUMI

HIERARCHY OF IDEAS AND "CHUNKING UP"

Human beings ultimately desire the same things. Regardless of race, religion, culture, country, geography, gender, sexuality, or beliefs, we share basic human needs, desires, challenges, and experiences. Before we can bridge worlds, it's essential to honor one another's maps and establish common ground. Then the finer points and details can be negotiated. In NLP, this negotiation model is known as the "hierarchy of ideas."

Since the human brain cannot process all the information we receive at any given time, we group information in chunks

or categories. We code, store, and label parts of the whole hier-
archically. Consider the category of transportation. There are
many methods of transportation. Each method could represent a smaller, "chunked down" category: planes, cars, bicycles,
boats, and canoes. We can select one of these categories and
chunk down further. If we chose planes, we could focus on Lear
jets, prop planes, commercial jetliners, and shuttles. We can
chunk down even further: commercial jetliners can be divided
into models such as the Airbus 320 or Boeing 747. Each of these
distinctions stems from the larger category.

  Without realizing it, Aqeela Sherrills used the "chunking"
technique and "hierarchy of ideas" to negotiate peace. He recognized the Bloods and Crips were each anchored in a very
"chunked down" map of the world—*you're red; we're blue.*
Aqeela "chunked up" and realized that both groups ultimately
wanted the same things: peace and power for their community,
honor, dignity, freedom, and security. He saw the colors red and
blue coming together to create purple, the color of royalty. He
illuminated how they could direct their energy toward building
a supportive community respecting life.

  The "chunking up" model as a technique for harmonizing
disparity and attaining agreement was based on studies of Milton Erickson, the father of modern hypnotherapy. Erickson was
a brilliant therapist who at age 17 contracted polio and became
paralyzed. During his paralysis, when he could use only his eyes
and ears to observe the world around him, Erickson became
acutely aware of subtleties in body language and nonverbal
communication.

  As a therapist, Erickson used this awareness to develop rapport with clients to create instantaneous positive change. He
realized ambiguous language patterns allowed him to bridge

worlds and create agreement. Ambiguous language, when used purposefully, minimizes the risk of clashing maps. This is why politicians speak in ambiguities; it induces a trancelike state that fosters agreement. A politician may say, "I'm working for the people to restore responsibility, honor, and integrity to the government to create positive change." It's a statement that sounds nice, and says nothing, but it's likely no one will dis-agree. In the realms of hypnosis and NLP, abstract language patterns that are artfully vague so as to match the clients experience are known as the "Milton model." The process of chunk-ing up for agreement is one of these language patterns.

You can chunk up for agreement by asking questions to discover the highest intent: *What does that behavior ultimately give you? How will it benefit you?* In the example of revenge, we chunked up to a high intent of security, freedom, and peace. If you chunk up high enough on any subject, you'll reach a place of unity and agreement. From this unified space, specifics can be more effectively negotiated.

Imagine that each of us, including our nations' leaders, negotiates details of agreements from a space of mutual respect, considering all points of view through a Supreme superposition. In this space, opposing energies harmonize. This is Supreme Influence in action. We communicate from the understanding: *we are one.* Leaders can use the hierarchy of ideas to negotiate peace among tribes and nations. Individuals can reach under-standing within families and communities. You can even use it in your meditation to unify fragmented aspects of *self.* Allow me to explain.

If you ever feel torn—as though a part of you wants one thing and another part of you wants something else—you can use the hierarchy of ideas to discover and appreciate the highest intent of each of these polarities. Perhaps part of you wants to be a stay-at-home mom, and the other part of you wants to be a powerful businesswoman; these seem conflicted. Recognizing and integrating these energies creates optimum conditions for Supreme Influence to flow. The part wanting to be a stay-at-home mom may be focused on love, while the part wanting to be a powerful businesswoman might seek freedom and success. When you recognize and honor the highest intent of all aspects of the multidimensional *you*, a solution presents itself; you realize you can indeed have it all. You can manifest love, freedom, and success in myriad harmonious, healthy ways. Essentially, the hierarchy of ideas is a process for inner alignment.

In life you command external influence when you have *inward fluency*, meaning you experience inner harmony. That's when your language, beliefs, focus, and physiology are aligned with your true purpose.

DISCOVER MAPS AND BRIDGE WORLDS

Suppose you are negotiating with someone who is anchored in a particular point of view, and your will is to bridge worlds. Center yourself. Discern the other person's intent beyond behavior. Discover what they *really* want. Use the Milton model and ask the person, *What does that behavior/situation give you? How does it benefit your life?* Chunk up! Activate your senses, become alert, listen and observe. Once you've discovered the person's ultimate aim (let's say it's power), you can then wield the meta-model (discussed in chapter 6) to discern new, specific, life-affirming ways for the person to experience power. You can continue to chunk up to discover the higher intent of power. In other words, when someone has power, what does that give him or her? What is the ultimate benefit of power? If you are sincere, have rapport, and keep chunking up, you will bridge worlds.

So, as you have just seen, in negotiations the Milton model allows you to chunk up, and the meta-model allows you to chunk down. Once you reach understanding, use the meta-model to negotiate finer points and determine the specifics of the agreement. Meta-model asks: *What specifically? How do you mean? How will you know?* Meta-model supports you in eliciting and discerning the details of someone's map of the world. Remember, meta-model requires rapport, or it appears invasive. Lighten up your energy and use linguistic softeners: *I'm wondering, what specifically . . . ? I'm curious, how do you mean . . . ?*

It's important to recognize that we each have our own unique ways of achieving the same ultimate goal. As we honor our individuality, appreciating the highest intent inspiring others' behaviors (even behaviors not in line with our own), we grow to understand the bigger picture and we can negotiate in a reasonable way, from a place of respect. This allows us to work in harmony to achieve mutually beneficial objectives. It opens creative channels, freeing our energy to innovate and consciously evolve.

WE ARE ONE

Though we live as individuals with our own strengths, desires, and challenges, we are all essentially one. Where does the air I breathe end and the air you breathe begin? The same life force flowing through you flows through me. The same Intelligence pulsing my heart is pulsing yours. At the end of the day, regardless of race, nationality, age, gender, or anything else seemingly "different," at the deepest level we want the same things: health, love, prosperity, freedom, and peace.

For my courses, I invite students to complete an in-depth questionnaire beforehand. I personally read each response. It's fascinating how often the answers intertwine and reveal patterns and universal desires and challenges. The common theme is: *How do we create prosperous lives that radiate health, authentic connection, self-love, a relationship with God or the Universe, freedom, personal power, and purpose?*

Each time I teach a course, someone will want to achieve a goal that another person in the same room has successfully accomplished. Resources and models of possibility surround us. I'll see a woman wanting to start a media company serendipitously sitting next to the CEO *of* one. The same woman might also be seeking a fulfilling intimate relationship, and sitting on her other side is a couple happily married for thirty years. That couple wants to learn tools to quantum-leap their finances, and they're sitting behind someone with a solid financial strategy and multiple profitable investments. The investor wants to improve his health and lose weight, and across the aisle sits a fitness expert, who is sitting next to a superhuman athlete. The athlete is seeking her purpose, and she'll be arm's length from a woman who happens to be an intuitive coach. And as it *is* in the reality of my course (microcosm), so it *is* in the reality of the Universe (macrocosm).

That which is below corresponds to
that which is above, and that which is above
corresponds to that which is below
to accomplish the miracle of the One.

—THE EMERALD TABLET, **HERMES TRISMEGISTUS**

Our strengths, desires, and challenges are mirrored in the kaleidoscope of people around us. Everything we think we *need* is present as we journey through the field of all possibility. What others may think they need, we can graciously offer. Every one of us has unique gifts to share in the present. We do not adventure alone. We are a tribal species, meant to live in cooperative community, so we may be allies and learn from the totality of our experience. Through conscious collaboration, we bridge gaps from where we are to where we choose to be.

Challenges arise. Miscommunications happen. It's part of being human. Individually we don't think the same, and we won't always agree, but we can experience harmony. We can see beyond the persistent illusion of separation into the Supreme breath animating all existence.

Living in Supreme Influence, we bring the fullness of our consciousness and talent to each moment. We cocreate spontaneous beauty and extraordinary value, uplifting all. To live in this unity requires that we open our eyes and hearts and acknowledge one another as one family on beloved Gaia, Mother Earth. As we honor our individuality and our oneness, we bridge worlds.

19

STATIC INTO DYNAMIC

You can never step into the same river twice,
for new waters are always flowing on to you.

—HERACLITUS OF EPHESUS

We inhale and exhale; seasons change; the tide ebbs and flows. Life is in constant motion. Relationships are in eternal flux. No-thing is static. Each moment is unique and sacred, one that has never been and never will be again. Sometimes, however, language can create the impression that something is static or that the past will dictate the present or future. This chapter is about speaking consciously, in the present moment. You will learn how to use your language to convert stuck states into dynamic states of presence and progressive action.

NOMINALIZATIONS AND THE ILLUSION OF STUCKNESS

In linguistics, a "nominalization" is when a noun (person, place, or thing) is used to represent a verb (an action word). A nominalization can create the illusion of "stuckness." If a wife said to her husband, "This relationship is a failure," the assumption would be the relationship could not be resurrected or transformed. The word *failure* is a nominalization—it eliminates choice, and assumes a static reality. Shifting the word *failure* to *failing*—although not the most empowering of terms—would create more options. If the relationship is in the process of failing, it's not dead yet; there's still hope.

How do you know if something is a nominalization?

A nominalization is a noun that *you cannot put in box*, not even a superhuge box. You create nominalizations when you take a *process* and make it seem unchanging. As we've seen, the word *failure* is a static nominalization; so are *love, growth,* and *success.* In contrast, *loving, growing,* and *succeeding* are dynamic action words. Terms with the suffixes *-ation, -ization,* or *-ism* are also nominalizations.

Suppose someone says, "There is no communication here." This statement is a *generalization* and also a *nominalization.* The dynamic process of "communicat*ing*" has been converted into a static noun. When someone makes such a statement, it's a clue that he is deleting and distorting reality. Examine the sentence. You'll notice that a lot of information has been left out. You can respond by using the meta-model to elicit the person's map while transforming the nominalization back into a verb. You might ask, "How do you mean? Who specifically isn't communicat*ing* with whom, about what?" or "How will you know when we are communicat*ing*?" Changing the word *communication* (a noun) into *communicating* (a verb) moves a static experience into an active process. Through this simple word shift, you can get the energy moving again. It's much easier to improve a situation when it's already in motion.

What is the nominalization in the following sentence? "I needed to get some reflection after I got that rejection letter from the committee." We actually have two nominalizations, the words *reflection* and *rejection*. The processes of *reflecting* and *rejecting* are dynamic, but this statement makes them seem fixed. Now visualize the difference in energy if this person said, "Since the committee initially chose not to accept my proposal, I've been *reflecting* on how I could improve it, and I'll be *resubmitting* it shortly."

Nominalizations can be limiting. For example, labeling a person as "ADD" (attention deficit disorder) is a nominalization. "ADD" is a noun—it is fixed. A person labeled this way might inadvertently accept this label as her identity, which in turn may stimulate the RAS to find information and experiences that confirm this statement. Remember, in previous chapters we discussed how the double-slit experiment, the observer effect, and the Pygmalion effect all confirm that how we observe and perceive people influences how they behave. People tend to live up to their names and titles. If someone acts in an *impulsive, distracted,* and/or *intensely active* way, this is his or her *behavior*; it is an action, not an absolute description of the person's identity. It's wiser to separate the behavior from the person. Living in Supreme Influence, you honor the person while supporting him or her in healing or transforming undesired behavior. Healing is an action. To create healing—to get unstuck—it is important to turn nominalizations back into processes.

In a universe of energy, where life is in constant motion, the idea of status quo is an illusion. There is only the present moment, and anything that appears "stuck" or "static" is really energy focused on the same thing over and over and over again. Right now, there are infinite possibilities available to you. Those possibilities are not available in the future or in the past. *Now* is the only moment there is.

Whatever you think about, you experience *as now*. For example, can you remember a time where you felt unstoppable? And as you think of a specific time right now, do you have a picture of that moment? Notice what you see, hear, and feel right now as you go back to that period, looking through your own eyes and feel the feelings of being unstoppable. As you think of that time right now, pay attention to what's happening in your body. How has your breathing changed? How has your posture shifted? Are there new sensations in your body? When is this happening? It's not happening in the past; it's happening now! Even as your mind drifts and wanders, your body is always, and only, right here in the present moment. If a rerun of the past plays in your mind, your body reexperiences it as now. When you imagine the future, your body experiences it this instant. Your power to create change exists in this eternal, unprecedented *now* moment.

20

STILLNESS AND SILENCE

When you lose touch with inner stillness,
you lose touch with yourself.
When you lose touch with yourself,
you lose yourself in the world.
Your innermost sense of self, of who you are,
is inseparable from stillness.
This is the 'I Am' that is deeper than name and form.

—ECKHART TOLLE

In my early twenties, I lived in Manhattan in a high-rise just outside one of New York City's busiest tunnels and streets. Noise surrounded me twenty-four hours a day. I could hear the honking of traffic, the bustling of people, the incessant clamor and commotion. Interestingly, during the early days of my evolution, at times I actually found it easier to drop into stillness in the midst of action. Perhaps it was because I grew up in a loud Cuban household where silence was rare. During this time I yearned for divine sacred union, and I intuitively knew the path was stillness. Every time I looked at a Buddha statue serenely sitting in lotus position, wise to the ways of the Universe, I knew . . . the answers reside in that still, silent space. The answers are not "out there"; they reside within. I wanted to know: *What unfolds in the silent void, and how can I experience it?*

The Buddha showed how through stillness, one is able to concentrate the mind and see with enlightened eyes. He recognized that meditation practices that work for one person do not necessarily work for another. He understood a technique guiding one individual into Nirvana could make another mad. Therefore, he taught different meditation techniques to different students according to each temperament.

During that time, I wanted to meditate like Buddha in serene silence, but due to a busy mind, I had all kinds of noisy thoughts running through my mental seas: *Am I doing this right? Am I in the gap yet? Oh no, that was a thought, I'm not in the gap, I'm still in my mind. Argh! Okay, get centered. Let go, let go, let go. Focus, Niurka! No, wait . . . don't focus—surrender! Yeah, surrender, I surrender. Breathe . . . inhale, exhale. Just let go of thought. Offer them up to the Divine. Ahhh, yes. That's right, I think I'm getting it now. I feel peace. Oh no, wait! I lost it. What happened? I was in the gap a moment ago. I think that was the gap. Argh!*

The problem was I was literally *looking* for stillness. Stillness isn't something you find, because stillness abides within you. It is an intrinsic, inseparable aspect of your infinite nature. Looking for stillness is like looking for the back of your head (without a mirror).

I was *searching* for the power and presence of the Divine, which can never be found in the level of consciousness that looks for it. Looking for something presupposes its absence, which becomes a self-fulfilling prophecy. What I mean is, looking for stillness leads to, well, looking for stillness. . . . You'll never find it that way.

Be still and know that I Am God.

−PSALMS 46:10

So there I was, running around in circles, in search of my illusive stillness. Soon after leaving New York, I decided to invest a month by myself in a meditation retreat center in the rain forests of Costa Rica. When I arrived I took a shuttle bus deep into the jungle and settled into my tree-house bungalow. I was inspired and ready to know the power and presence of God as a very real and nonfleeting experience, with no distractions. The next morning, I woke refreshed after a good night's sleep. I made tea and sat with the intent of transcending my mind. I told myself, *I will not eat breakfast until I meditate for at least one hour.* I looked at the clock: it was 6:45 a.m. I closed my eyes. A few moments passed and I peeked: 6:47 a.m. I took a deep breath and closed my eyes again. Feeling unsettled, I opened them: 6:48 a.m. Argh! The longer I sat, the more frustrated I became. The more frustrated I became, the more disappointed I became in myself and the more agitated my mind grew.

All men's troubles stem from not being
able to sit in a room alone.

—BLAISE PASCAL

Exasperated, committed, and hopeful, I went to see the retreat center's yoga instructor. She suggested I attend her dynamic meditation class that afternoon. She said it worked wonders for busy Western minds.

I attended her class. This was my first group meditation class. There were only a handful of people, and the instructor began with a brief introduction. "Today, you will learn dynamic meditation," she explained, "a practice to transcend the chattering mind and come into stillness." Her description made me smile. *It's going to happen right now . . . I'm going to slip into the gap!* I thought. She continued: "It lasts one hour, has three stages, and we'll have music playing in the background." First we were instructed to vigorously shake our bodies for twenty minutes, as intensely as we could, without any consideration for our surroundings. Let go, shake, explode, allow the energy to move through your body unobstructed. "Be in your own experience," she explained. "This is about you, not anybody else." Then we were guided to dance freely and let our spirits be wild for another twenty minutes. Finally we were asked to sit in silence and focus our concentration on the space between our eyebrows, which she described as the third eye, or "Ajna," the eye of intuition.

I participated wholeheartedly. By the time I sat for the final twenty minutes of silent meditation, I became weightless, as though I was floating. I was *still, without thought.* Then a gong awakened my quiet universe. I came out of meditation realizing I had been still for an infinite twenty minutes.

I left class inspired. This was the first time I "meditated" for that long without opening my eyes to look at the clock once! I entered the gap! I walked down to the beach, elated and grateful. The sun was going down, and there was a sailor's sky filling the heavens above with hues of reds, pinks, and gold. I walked along the shore, feeling the warmth of the sun's rays caressing my body, the wind dancing through my hair, and the wet, hot sand beneath my feet. I saw fishermen casting their lines, and a man climbing a coconut tree with a machete. Everything was still, and I was the witness. I sat on an uprooted tree and observed. Soon the sun had set, and I realized I was sitting serenely; my being was still. There was no thought. I sat in this awareness, experiencing the Supreme mystical sacred union I yearned for all along. It was already within me; it was all around me.

There was nothing to seek, nothing to find. There was only presence, the sweet awareness of life itself, the mystical manifestation of divine energy dancing in the fire of love. The search was over. The maya, or illusion, dissolved. The Supreme kingdom is here. I Am here.

BE STILL AND KNOW THAT I AM

The source of your presence and power is stillness. Self-realization, living your purpose, and fulfilling your destiny—the seeds of these *are* available to you now in the calm, silent space within the sanctuary of your own being. In stillness you experience the qualities of your soul—*sat, chit, ananda*—which in Sanskrit means love, knowingness, and bliss. All manifest reality came into being from this tranquil and transcendental void. Physical matter is born from the womb of stillness. This is the space from which God spoke, "Be light!" This is how you access your creative powers, the infinite "I am" within you. It is from stillness that you speak into existence through the authority of Logos.

Each of us is one with the Supreme. We can call it God, a Higher Power, Nature, Great Spirit, Universal Law, or whatever we choose. All great religions point to One essence, which has been assigned many names by different traditions. Dr. Wayne Dyer says, "You cannot get wet from the word *water*." This means it doesn't matter what word we use to describe water; the energetic substance "water" is what it is despite our labels. And so it is with the Supreme. Different cultures honor the One Source in different ways and with different names and symbols. However, there is one portal through which we can all directly access Supreme Being—stillness. Stillness is the silent space unifying all existence.

Through stillness, you experience sacred union. Without it, there is static on the line and your god call gets dropped due to poor reception. Stillness keeps the airways and channels open and clear. Through stillness, you become available to the divine evolutionary impulse, which is seeking to express a unique aspect of its infinite nature through you and is unique to you alone. This is *your* rare gift, *your* purpose in this life, your sacred duty. Your intuitive wisdom grows as you honor, welcome, and allow stillness to be the nucleus of every thought, every word, and every deed.

Through stillness, you know your *self* as whole and complete. There are no unfulfilled needs or desires in stillness. Here your mind and body are calm and relaxed. Hence, you are open and able to receive. Dropping into stillness nourishes you; it deepens you. Your answers reside here—in the silence within the sanctum of your own heart. There are no boundaries in the still, silent space—*you* are in eternity. This is the fertile realm of pure potential where everything is possible.

How easily can you tune in to your own inner stillness? Perhaps you can vividly remember a time when you felt timeless, absolutely still, beyond thought, simply aware and calm. This is the void, the still, silent space before the beginning of time, from which all existence emerged. Stillness is the Source of the cosmos itself. The same stillness residing in the cosmos is the stillness within you. It is the infinite space from which you download divine wisdom, which begets understanding. Within stillness is the sea of all possibilities. In this void is *no-thing*, no thoughts, no words, no matter, only the eternal bliss of being. Stillness is the primordial nothingness from which language, creation, and answers emerge. It's not really "nothing." It's the fullness of infinite potential. It's "no-thing."

Silence supports you in accessing stillness, but you do not *need* silence to be still. Silence is the absence of noise, whereas stillness is a state of being. Both silence and stillness are intertwined. But you can absolutely experience stillness in the absence of silence. You can tune in to the silence that is the backdrop from which all noise emerges.

MEDITATION PRACTICES
FOR ACCESSING STILLNESS

Meditating in the rain forest awakened me to new dimensions of understanding. The forest was filled with sounds of nature—birds chirping, monkeys howling "oo-oo-oo-aa-aa-oo," crickets chirping, frogs croaking, parrots squawking, and myriad other sounds plucking the notes of nature's sacred song. In the midst of the infinitude of sound, I experienced the most profound stillness. I was aware of the silent space, the backdrop upon which all creation sings its melody in adoration to the Divine.

Meditation offers the ultimate opportunity to clear and calm your mind, bringing your consciousness to the present, allowing you to move purposefully toward your vision. Meditation creates fertile soil in the mind for positive seeds of action to flourish. Each one of us is inherently capable of realizing enlightened states of consciousness in our lifetime. Everything you see reflected during meditation grows within you individually and influences our collective consciousness. Meditation is the act of polishing the mirror that is a reflection of your life. It opens the heart, quiets the mind, and creates the space to listen with deeper care to the guidance of your divine inner compass.

There are many ways to access enlightenment. Like Buddha understood, different methods suit different personalities. This is phenomenal news, because it means we each have the freedom to select the techniques that resonate most within us! Traditional practices of the East tend to favor quiet contemplation and silent meditation. In the West the dominant culture and environment has been more active. For many people in the West, it has been easier to access stillness through action. This is the Zen, which flows through virtuoso music, art, film, dance, literature, and sports. When there is much activity in the periphery, some people find it easier to concentrate.

It's not important which technique you use to slip into the infinite space beyond thought. Different people access the same stillness in different ways. Whether you sit in silent meditation or mindfully engage in purposeful action without attachment, what is important is that you discover a method that works for you and consistently practice it.

Athletes often refer to this state of grace as "being in the zone." When an athlete is in the zone, she loses identification with ego, the sense of "I and me" being separate from others. In these inspired moments, the athlete transcends time and space. She is in eternity, and the Creative Powers flow through unobstructed. Superhuman feats are accomplished in this dimension. This is why our culture invests so much money and time in sports . . . through the presence under pressure that athletes experience, we touch the eternal. When we see others reach a zenith—where everything becomes a fluid dance, fully expressed, alive, and powerful—it ignites infinite possibility within us.

The stillness in stillness is not the real stillness;
only when there is stillness in movement
does the universal rhythm manifest.

—BRUCE LEE

Where in your life do you feel this way? Where do you touch the timeless and eternal? Is it playing sports? Being in nature? Making love? Is it in your life's work? With your family? Creating art? Tune in and become aware of where you currently experience stillness. Since stillness is omnipresent, you can access it in every moment through limitless channels. Conscious breathing, meditating, physical exercise, lovemaking, playing music, writing poetry, visualizing, communing with nature, arranging flowers, surrendering deeply into anything which brings you joy or expresses your creativity: these are all ways you can experience stillness, the holy space from which masterpieces are born.

Why do some people travel to sacred lands and holy places? Why do some seek out spiritual teachers or enlightened masters? These places and people can accelerate the awakening of consciousness. Mystics know that being in the presence of an enlightened master can initiate a student into expanded realms of understanding, so long as the student is receptive and ready. Being in the presence of an awakened one or in holy land that carries the frequency of centuries of devoted meditation creates the conditions for you to more deeply drop into stillness.

If you've found it difficult to enter the gap, the space between thoughts, mindfully go into nature and simply become aware of silence. Notice it. You don't need to do anything, just be aware. Through mindful awareness you access stillness within. Look at a flower, listen to a running stream, climb a mountain, sit by a tree, walk on the sand by the ocean. These expressions of nature inspire awe and wonder. They have the power to teach you stillness.

WHAT IS SILENCE?

God's one and only voice is silence.

—HERMAN MELVILLE

Silence gives words their weight. Without silent space, communication is just noise. What would happen if you played all the keys on the piano at once? You couldn't distinguish the individual notes. There would be no rhythm, no harmony, no accentuation of a single, beautiful sound. It would be . . . chaos. It's the space between the notes that makes the music. Anyone can play notes. The key to mastery is inflecting those notes with space. The virtuosos of the world don't just play music. They play the silence, feeling the cadences, hearing the fullness in the emptiness.

When you honor the silent space between thoughts, between words, you join infinity. From here you speak into existence with purpose, poise, precision, and power, and the Universe lovingly responds to your congruent command. Knowing when to harness your energy and when to pull back is as important as knowing the wisest thing to say. Masters of Supreme Influence have the awareness and discernment to know when it's the wisest choice to speak and when it's smarter to be silent, observe, and listen.

Living in Supreme Influence, you reside in stillness, and you speak from this calm, centered state of being, regardless of whether or not there is silence.

In silence there is eloquence.
Stop weaving and see how the pattern improves.
—RUMI

TWO SIDES OF ONE COIN: SILENCE AND PURPOSEFUL SPEECH

I often regret that I have spoken;
never that I have been silent.
—PUBLILIUS SYRUS

Deliberate speech and purposeful silence are two sides of one coin. They create tension and release, which inspires action. They are perfect complements in cosmic balance, like yin and yang. Practiced together in harmony, they exponentially increase your ability to create on purpose. If you talk too much; you give away your power. It's not authentic to talk too much; it's undisciplined. If you speak too little, you don't honor your truth. Supreme Influence balances conscious communication with intentional pauses. Equilibrium is key to accessing the fullness of your creative powers.

We are masters of the unsaid words,
but slaves of those we let slip out.
—WINSTON CHURCHILL

Investing a moment to mindfully pause before you speak or send an e-mail or a text attunes you with your intuitive guidance system. It saves you from blunders and miscreation (not creating on purpose). This is the reason why enlightened masters have taught that the greatest action is often inaction, or not taking misguided action. It's not just what you say or do that makes a positive difference—sometimes it's what you *don't* say or do.

In Taoism, there is a concept known as "wu-wei," which teaches action through inaction, as an expression of natural law. Wu-wei illumines that everything in the Universe has a natural rhythm, a divine order. When you align with this rhythm, you "do" without "doing." Your actions become natural expressions of your spirit guided by your inner knowing. Wu-wei describes a form of intuitive cooperation with the natural order of the Universe, which unfolds in perfect harmony when allowed to organically manifest without the interference of ignorant human thinking and speaking.

Stillness isn't something you have to go get. It's not something you do. You experience stillness when you stop making yourself "do" and allow yourself to "be." Here the concept of "trying" is nonexistent. You don't have to think about blinking or breathing. You don't have to exert effort for the hair on your head to grow, or for the blood to pump through your veins, or for your food to digest. These natural rhythms happen without conscious thought or *doing*. You don't have to wonder where your next breath will come from, or guess if the sun will rise tomorrow. You can trust these processes to beat to their own regular and steady pulse. The moment you surrender and trust that Supreme presence surrounds you in stillness—this is the moment you arrive. Stillness is what always exists, everywhere, beyond noise and chatter.

Although silence can sometimes support you in concentrating, it's not necessary to run to nature or sequester yourself in a meditation room to find silent space. It's as simple as centering your body, attuning your focus, listening to the sound of your breath, or becoming aware of the rhythm of your heart.

Be mindful. Invite pauses. Invest a moment to be still before *any* action. If you launch an e-mail or a text, inhale two deep breaths before you press Send. What is spoken cannot be unspoken. It's wise to disconnect for a moment from the hustle and bustle to contemplate the most effective way to communicate and bridge worlds. You can ask, *Does this clearly convey what I authentically want to say?*

You may not always have conscious control over what your eyes see or what your ears hear, but you do have the ability to choose what leaves and enters your mouth. Your mouth is a gate, and it's wise to be discerning with what crosses this threshold. When you speak, be careful; ensure your words communicate your genuine intent. When you eat or drink or otherwise ingest or inhale, be mindful that what you consume nourishes your body, mind, and spirit. You can ask questions: *What is the healthiest choice? How can I tune in to my intuitive wisdom right now? How can I communicate with clarity and kindness? How can I speak my truth while honoring their truth?* Ultimately, if you only speak truth, then everything you say will be true.

When words are scarce
they are seldom spent in vain.
—WILLIAM SHAKESPEARE

CALMING THE MIND AND DISCERNING YOUR AUTHENTIC VOICE

Once while traveling, I experienced a titanic miscommunication with a friend. The trip was a bit of a whirlwind, and I rushed to the airport without resolving the issue. Everything was moving rapidly, and it wasn't until the plane took off that I had the opportunity to think. As I sat in my seat, mulling over what transpired, I found myself becoming angry, then furious. I began breathing deeply to calm my state. But my mind was agitated and racing. I decided to write my friend a letter. I took out my laptop and let the flood of thoughts rampaging my being release onto the page. My fingers were on fire. My angered thoughts poured like lava gushing from an exploding volcano. Suddenly the woman seated next to me turned and sweetly asked, "Are you an author?"

"Actually, I'm writing a letter to a friend," I replied.

"I write a lot as well," she said. She went on to tell me that she was completing her PhD. Her thesis was on the teachings of the Taoist sage Lao Tzu, based on wisdom extrapolated from Korean picture books. I chuckled, as I thought, *Of course you are; there are no coincidences.* I had studied the Tao Te Ching and the teachings of Lao Tzu for years, and I knew in that moment that I was not vibing in alignment with my Higher self.

I looked at her and intuitively knew she was a vessel for Spirit to deliver a message. I listened as she described her studies. I asked, "If you were to encapsulate your entire thesis into one sentence, what would it be?"

She gazed at me softly and said, *"Do not disturb."*

"Do not disturb? How do you mean?" I asked, looking at her.

"Yes. If you want peace in your life, do not disturb. Do not do things that will cause disturbance in others, because if you do, you will breed unhappiness within you."

Her message landed in my universe like a God bomb. It was poignant and timely. I knew in that moment that if I would've hit the Send button, that e-mail letter would have caused a major disturbance in my friend and within me. My neighbor explained how suffering is the effect of making poor choices, and a poor choice is one that disturbs others. Every cause has an effect, she added, and inflicting pain on others *always* returns to us because we are all connected, and everything is energy.

"This is why it is wise to be still and consider the effects of our actions before we speak or send e-mails or texts," she concluded.

"Thank you," I said. I deleted the letter and closed my laptop.

Notice the gap between breaths, the space between heartbeats. Stillness permeates this gap. It is the infinite backdrop on which creation happens. Look at this page. The words on the page are set on a clean, white background. A painting is painted on a clean, fresh canvas. This blank canvas is stillness. It is the arena in which we create the masterpieces of our lives. If the page is muddy or cloudy, we cannot properly or powerfully create. And so it is in life.

If your mind is turbulent or unsettled, you lose touch with the Creative Powers. If you throw a pebble into turbulent waters, what happens? Not a lot. Even if you throw a huge rock in, the influence will be minimal. Conversely, if you throw a pebble into calm, still waters, the waves ripple out endlessly. It is the same with your mind. Your mind is like an infinitely expansive sea.

If your mind is agitated, your perceptions become distorted, and your ability to effectively communicate diminishes. Making decisions with an unsettled mind breeds destruction. If you experience a disturbance, honor it and observe. Project your consciousness into third position and become the "observer," as discussed in chapter 16. Breathe through the disturbance, knowing this too shall pass, and as you do, pay attention to the gap between breaths. When your mind is calm and still, your focused intent is carried out with less interference, and it will manifest.

Your intuitive wisdom is continually flowing, just like the sun is consistently shining. At times there may be clouds in the way, creating the very persistent illusion of gloom. However, beyond the veils reigns the light. A disturbed mind engenders cloudiness, creates interference, and blocks the downpour of divine energy. But nonetheless Supreme wisdom continually flows. It is simply not discernible because the channels are not yet open. Stillness opens the gates to Supreme knowledge. When your mind is still, you have an infinite blank canvas on which to pour the magnificence of your unique gifts for all to enjoy. A calm mind has tremendous power to materialize your evolutionary intent.

Through stillness, you enter into communion with Source. As you honor stillness, you discern your authentic voice. You become a vessel for the Creative Powers to move through. I once asked my beloved friend Michael Beckwith, "How do you meditate?" He said, "I become still and available to Spirit."

When you are still, you become a channel of Supreme light and love. This is the space where you receive intuitive wisdom and allow insights to naturally be translated into action through you. Different people access their intuition in different ways. It can come as a subtle sensation, a knowing, a soft whisper, a dream, an image in your mind's eye, a supernatural feeling, or something else. Spirit delights in manifesting through you in myriad ways, often appearing as meaningful "coincidences."

Stillness opens you to the gifts of the Universe and allows for conversation rather than just a one-way pronouncement. It's a dialogue, even a love affair, with the world around you. All great heroes have conversations with the supernatural. Arjuna was guided by Krishna, Luke Skywalker trusted the Force, Joan of Arc heard the voice of God in her ear, and you too have access to Universal Intelligence through stillness. Become intimate and talk with the Supreme. Listen for guidance. If something catches your attention, consider the Supreme is speaking directly to you.

Living in stillness, you connect with your creativity, allowing your authentic voice to grow clearer and stronger. This voice speaks with love. Trusting this inner voice above all, you cease old repetitive patterns and instead download fresh ideas and original insights. Inspiration comes through stillness. You produce superior results when you speak from a calm, centered, focused, still space.

Stillness is a way of life. It is an internal posture. In stillness, you experience certainty even in the midst of uncertainty. Regardless of what arises, you remain centered and unidentified. You will find that the more you cultivate inner stillness, the more attractive you become. Others will be drawn to you. Your eyes will allure as they beam with wisdom of the ages.

Through stillness you access genius and experience epiphanies. Stillness allows you to cultivate trust in your inner voice and courage in your choices. Insights for your evolution are hidden within stillness, like treasure awaiting discovery. Stillness is where you source wisdom to know *your self*, love *your life*, and live *your purpose*.

RELAX AND HONOR GESTATION

On the earthly plane, we navigate the realms of time and space. Our vision doesn't always manifest instantaneously. Sometimes, when we cast the pebble of our intent, it takes time, and maybe a little distance, before the essence of our aspiration materializes. Sometimes it takes hours, days, weeks, even months for your creations to fully form. A receptive womb takes time to nurture a baby, bring it to maturity, and welcome it into the world. It is the same with your creations. Once you've planted the seeds of your intention, let nature take its course. If you plant seeds in your garden, you must give them time and space to grow. If you dig them up the next day to check on how they're doing, they won't mature. Depending on the nature of your creations, they too need to develop, to become ripe before manifesting. Enjoy the space nestled between the moment you cast your intention and the moment your dreams come to fruition. Be still, and silently trust all is unfolding in divine order.

BE OPEN TO RECEIVE

Life fills a receptive vessel. Consider nature. Water flows to the ocean, filling caverns and cavities; sand crabs make homes in open seashells; babies grow in a mother's womb. Life requires a friendly host. A chaotic, cluttered, or full container cannot receive life. You can only pack so much into a space, and the open, receptive space is what gives a container its value. A vase is useful because it has space to hold flowers and water. Without space, it could not fulfill its purpose.

> We put thirty spokes together and call it a
> wheel, but it is on the space where there
> is nothing that the usefulness of the wheel
> depends. We turn clay to make a vessel, but it
> is on the space where there is nothing that the
> usefulness of the vessel depends. We pierce
> doors and windows to make a house, and it is
> on these spaces where there is nothing that the
> usefulness of the house depends. Therefore
> just as we take advantage of what is, we should
> recognize the usefulness of what is not.
>
> —LAO TZU

The Universe beams light and life. It continually offers to impregnate you with seeds of your highest possibility. There are only two prerequisites: a receptive, loving womb and the vibrational equivalent within your own being. Your heart's desires surround you, so long as you remain aware and open. If you run your hands beneath a faucet, you will catch the water when your hands are relaxed and cupped. If your hands are clenched in constricted fists, you cannot contain the flow. And so it is with life. You will be filled to the degree that you are open and receptive.

STILLNESS HEALS

Stillness heals. Simply holding space for someone can be a miraculous gift. Rather than giving advice, teaching, or trying to fix something—just listen, be present, and allow. See and receive someone with open arms, loving eyes, and attentive ears. Connect with your beloveds on a soul level. Look into their eyes and see past personality. Discover the essence that animates their being. Recognize this encounter as holy—spirit meeting spirit, through you.

The Supreme is Spirit. Therefore, it can manifest only through nature and humans. The Supreme requires a receptive vessel to manifest in the kingdom of Earth. Although inherent within everyone, these Creative Powers remain latent until one is awake, receptive, and still.

IMAGINE ALL THE PEOPLE

Have you ever shared a moment of silence with a crowd? It's a sacred experience to commune in silence. It's an act of reverence, and it gives a sense of gravity and honor to the occasion.

Our world is moving rapidly now through advances in technology and information flooding us on the Internet. It could be easy to be overwhelmed by the frenzied activity of a changing world. Therefore, it is essential to cultivate inner stillness. Imagine a world where each person honors stillness and values the quality of their own vibration. Imagine how much clarity and peace we can create in our world as each one of us chooses to be mindful before speaking and cognizant before acting.

Let us punctuate this moment in our history with a moment of stillness: a period, a full pause—a rest from the busy doings or the tendency to fix or undo what has been done. Let us collectively take a breath, let go of our thoughts, and enter the gap. Let's appreciate the no-thing that exists before the some-thing. As we drop into stillness, we source the wisdom and power to consciously create what is to come.

21

SAILING THE INFINITE
SEA OF LOVE

How often have you sailed in my dreams.
And now you come in my awakening,
which is my deeper dream.
Ready am I to go, and my eagerness
with sails full set awaits the wind.

—KAHLIL GIBRAN

Two millennia ago, a child was born in Bethlehem. He walked among us and became King. But he was more than a man or a King; he knew himself as *God*. He offered us the keys to create Heaven on Earth, but many weren't ready. Much of the deeper wisdom of his teaching was lost in translation.

Two millennia before that, a man was born a prince. He walked among us and became enlightened. He too discovered he could be more than just a man, and he recognized his godly nature. He asked life's most essential questions: *Who am I? What's my purpose? Why am I here?* He shared profound knowledge and answers to these riddles, and yet many weren't ready. Much of his teaching was misunderstood.

In this millennia, a man was born a genius. He walked among us and was passionately curious. He became inspired by how a compass points magnetic north. Intuitively, he knew an invisible force, presumed as empty space, guided the needle, and he embarked to discover it. He asked transcendental questions, unlocked secrets to time and space, and was honored as the most influential person of the century. Much of his wisdom was misused and not understood.

The answers have always been here.

Now we are ready.

For centuries, enlightened masters like Jesus and Buddha and geniuses such as Einstein have illumined how we are divine beings blessed with freedom to choose and power to create. We live in a universe of infinite possibility that matches the vibration of our thought. We are emanating our reality into existence through our *vibe*.

Now we are becoming more aware of this knowledge. We are becoming even more conscious of how to positively influence our world through words, actions, and energetic intent. Enlightened masters have prophesized this coming of age since the beginning of mankind's story. In the great stories, as Saint Athanasius, the twentieth bishop of Alexandria, wrote, "God became man so men might become gods." This is the opportunity at hand, for each one of us to be:

A pure and available conscious vessel for the Divine evolutionary impulse to flow unobstructed.

We are all unique emanations of the Supreme Source of all existence. As we come into unity with the essence of divinity within, we come into unity with one another. We grow our global community to nurture, support, and advance our next stage of evolution. Together we consciously create our world as we want it to be.

In this new reality, *you* are the chosen one. *You* are the one who will answer life's most essential questions: *Who am I? Why am I here? What's my purpose? How will I fulfill my destiny?* When *you* are ready to receive answers, they come. Your evolution elevates the consciousness of the planet. Rise and own your inheritance. Stand firm in your creative powers.

SEE THROUGH DIVINE EYES

It takes vision and courage to see through *what is* into *what could be*. If you look at a cord of wood, you don't see its potential as fire with your physical eyes. You must transcend the obvious and look from a deeper place. A shaman once told me, "You don't see oil in a coconut, but it is there." In other words, discovering the magical realm requires vision *and* a process; extracting fire from wood requires both vision and purposeful action. It is essential to unify science and spirituality. You never see God with your physical eyes, but God is everywhere, just like the fire in the wood. Living in Supreme Influence, you see through divine eyes and develop a consistent practice to create value and beauty according to your unique talents. This is the journey we are on together.

God comes to us veiled under the appearance
of bread! We see him, we touch him,
we taste him, we eat him, and his eternity
trembles within our mortal flesh.

—ELIPHAS LEVI

THE MAGIC OF STORYTELLING

Storytelling is an ancient art with the power to heal. Elders and wise ones share stories with their tribes to carry on tradition and awaken understanding. I love storytelling, both sharing and hearing.

Once while traveling on sacred adventure, I became friends with a guru. In the East, *guru* is an affectionate term for "teacher." My friend Guru is a beautiful, simple, straightforward man who lives with his family in the countryside of Bali. We connected deeply, like soul kin, and he gave me a precious gift—a story. Not just any story, but the kind that penetrates deep into your being, causing you to remember *who you are* and *why you are here*.

It was almost midnight, and the air was cool and crisp. Guru's traditional Balinese home was mostly outdoors. He lived on a rice field, and I could hear the irrigation water flowing like a small river. We sat on a red mat covering the house's concrete floor. In the background an orchestra of frogs croaked a harmonious song of nature. The stars were shining. I could see the waxing moon hovered over Guru's head like a light emerging from his crown chakra.

He looked at me with piercing brown eyes. His face relaxed as he sat comfortably in lotus position, his belly slightly round like a happy Buddha. He wore a black sarong with a checkerboard sash and black headdress. He was not merely a spiritual teacher; he was a *balian*—a supernatural healer. The town's people loved and revered him.

He began his story. His tone was commanding. He spoke with authority and precision. His physiology was masterfully congruent with his words and intent. It was as though he packed the force of the whole universe in a single syllable. I became silent, anticipating what he would say next. With deliberate intent, he articulated an intense flow of lyrical Indonesian. I understood only a few words between his notes. His body language and tonality revealed infinitely more than the words I could decrypt. Deciphering the *balian's* teaching was a bit like decoding hieroglyphics.

Serendipitously, our friend Wijana, the keeper of the local temple, was with us. Wijana is a spiritual man who spends his days in meditation, prayer, and service. He also speaks English fairly well and has a unique way of expressing himself. Every time he finishes a sentence, he authentically smiles from ear to ear. You can't help but smile with him. As the *balian* and I would speak, Wijana would do his best to translate. When Wijana didn't know a word, I would quickly look it up on the Internet. There were times I could intuit the translation wasn't 100 percent accurate. During those moments, I would continue asking questions in myriad ways until I concluded we achieved understanding. All three of us were committed to communicating, and together we found a way—through words, voice cues, emotional intensity, drawings, technology, and love—to bridge worlds.

Here's my rendition of the story the *balian* shared with me that night and many nights to follow. This story evolved in our conversations, as we each contributed hues and dimensions to make it come alive. This story is about *you.*

> You *are sailing through the infinite sea of existence. You have your boat, helm, and three sails to guide you to your chosen island. The three sails are named* idep *(pure thought),* sabda *(pure word), and* bayu *(pure action).*

Wake up. Embark! Decide to which island you will voyage
in the sea of infinite possibility. Then, sail! If you want
to touch God, you must be in inspirited action. Without
action, you do not see God, because God is like fire inside
the wood, like oil in the coconut. If you can see the island,
even clearly, and desire to travel there, without action noth-
ing happens. Still your mind and set out to sea.

Regardless of conditions or weather, center your being,
observe your compass, look through your telescope, and
begin to sail. You experience balance in your body as long
as you focus and take purposeful action. Sail toward the
destination of your choosing, using your helm to navigate
between the energies of left and right, yin and yang, dark-
ness and light. Know the sea encompasses all possibilities,
and you ride upon its waves. Concentrate your vision and
stay centered as you continue toward the island of your
highest calling. Your course is set; your direction is clear.
Your heading is visible in the distance, and your vision is not
swayed by sea conditions or anything else.

You sail through the sea of light and shadow, without
attachment, because in the physical world there is no escap-
ing darkness. Light and shadow exist side by side. They
are complementary, like masculine and feminine, high and
low, hot and cold. This is the way of the manifest universe,
the ebb and flow of all existence, and you are at peace with
this understanding for your consciousness resides in eternal
light. Thus your essence is unscathed.

As you sail you are not attached to one side of the hull
or the other, for that would bring imbalance. You under-
stand the rhythm of life. Everything unfolds in seasons.
Spring follows winter, and you let go of the past, integrating

its gifts and blessing it as you move forward. You have seen much, and like Buddha you recognize the inevitability of pain. However, you view things differently now. You see through enlightened eyes, looking upon all creation with Supreme light. You are compassionate toward hardship, and not phased by it. Even in the midst of fog, your perception clears.

Ultimately, you witness the moment, smile, and move on. You are not identified. You are not defined or bound by material things. You understand impermanence, life, and love. You are free!

You are aware, and you sail. Your journey is eternal, and thus you continue navigating the infinite sea of possibilities, traveling from island to island.

Rise and raise your sails, use your compass to chart your course. Your grandest vision can certainly be achieved. You must concentrate and focus. You have the power to direct your mind. You do this by claiming your creative powers and aligning your sails: idep (pure thinking), sabda (pure speaking), and bayu (pure action)—this is inward fluency. This is the discipline for the realization of excellence. This is the Supreme superpower of a human being.

Your mind has supernatural powers. It can travel beyond the planets into the cosmos. It is wider than the entire universe. You can be anywhere in the world and instantly transmit your mind to another destination. Your mind has no limits, just like the infinite sea. You must monitor your mind and properly direct it. Learn to guide your mind through deliberate practice. You accomplish this by becoming still, allowing inspirited action to flow through you as you sail. You are alert and conscious of keeping the vessel balanced. You understand that in the absence of balance, you can get lost at sea. Therefore, with love in your heart, you focus and summon all your resources to properly position your sails as you cruise toward your destination, which holds the next grand adventure.

You are awake and aware. You are attuned to the forces of nature and live in sacred union with the Universe. Your vessel does not fall off or heave to; it will only move windward. You simply align your sails to catch the power of the wind and take voyage in a boat named Astha-Brata.

ASTHA-BRATA: SUPREME POWERS OF BEING

I sat entranced as I listened to the *balian* share his portrayal of the tale of the *Astha-Brata*. In the Ramayana, a classical Sanskrit epic of India believed to have been written between the fourth and second centuries BC, there's a story about a battle between a Hindu deity named Sri Rama, the King of Ayodhya, and Ravana, the King of Lanka, also known as the ten-headed demon king. Rama killed Ravana in a great battle for capturing and imprisoning his wife. As the story is told, after Ravana's death, Rama crowned Ravanna's younger brother, Vibhishana, as succeeding King of Lanka. The advice that Rama gave to Vibhishana on how to be a powerful and just ruler has become one of the most influential passages from Javanese literature. It is a leadership philosophy with eight principles based on the wisdom of the natural Universe, and it is known as "Astha-Brata."

As I captured every word of the story, still reading between the lines, the *balian* explained how the forces of nature exist with your own being—the sun, the moon, the earth, the wind, the fire, the water, and the stars. These natural forces of the universe, which existed eons before the origin of mankind, come together to form your being as well as all manifest existence. They abide within you; they are one with you. Every aspect of your nature is composed of these essential building blocks of life. They are teachers, and they offer you profound wisdom, surrounding and emanating from within you as you sail the infinite sea toward the island of your vision.

You radiate the essence of Ra, the Sun who majestically shines on all existence equally, giving absolutely to all, without reservation. Like Ra, you give unconditionally, with no expectation. Emanating light is your nature. You are a source of light and life. You brighten the way for all who sail the sea, and you warm their bodies. All creation awakens and blooms in your warm embrace. You don't hold back. You are consistent, dependable, and steadfast. Everywhere you go, you bestow life. You are a source of pure power, emanating the radiant light of Helios. Your supreme light awakens the dawn, greeting each day and each moment anew.

You mirror the qualities of Luna, the Moon, a soft energy full of love. You light and guide the way. As darkness falls upon the sea, you reflect a gentle glow, attracting loving spirits that accompany you. You glimmer a mysterious brightness as you sail this infinite journey of sacred reflection. You understand the cycles of nature and trust your intuitive guidance. As you travel, your beauty expands and the natural world brightens to your presence.

You stand firm in the abundance of Gaia, Mother

Earth, *who is solid and resolute, able to receive all, the light and the shadow. As you voyage you offer your cornucopia of gifts without discrimination to those you encounter. You are grounded and generous. You reap what you sow and bring things through to fruition. Through your presence you cultivate the friendly space where all can stand and grow. You share and live in thanksgiving. All is renewed in your presence.*

You wield the Wind, *the prana, the breath, which exists everywhere. You inhale and exhale, fueling your sails and supporting your fellow sailors in further realizing their vision. The same breath breathing you breaths all—there is only one breath, one wind. You are free to move in all directions. You carry the spirit of air, lifting and inspiring. You consciously create atmosphere, bestowing zephyrs, which purify minds, and currents, which elevate spirits. Your natural momentum propels you toward your destiny gliding upon the winds of change, allowing, letting go, and trusting Supreme guidance to set the course as you surrender into the breath of life.*

You transmit the Fire *of life within you, the eternal flame, the Supreme spark, which reveals the invisible forces behind all manifestation. You carry the torch of illumination, the visible and invisible flame, which burns through ignorance and lights the path of truth, granting knowledge. You believe in others and encourage with optimism and enthusiasm. You emit warmth, gathering your beloveds round the sacred fire for stories and nourishment on the island of your choosing. You cook the remnants of sacrifice, offering the fruits of your actions unto the Highest. Your fire ignites the simmering embers fueling your creative powers,*

and you take confident and assertive action toward your
vision. You burn bridges of past disillusionments and sur-
render; like the mystical phoenix, you dance in the flames,
allowing the forces of nature to consume the past and create
fertile ground for new life.

You encompass the powers of Water. *Your depth is*
unknown. Your cup eternally fills, refreshes, and quenches
the thirst of all who surround you. The fluid energy in
your being transforms static pools of existence into waves
of forward movement, cleansing and purifying nonevolved
awareness into crystalline oceans of creative abundance.
Your spirit moves freely. If problems arise, you grace-
fully engulf and transform them into opportunities. You
surmount all obstacles, allowing the flow of life to guide
the way. You encompass the roaring expanse of infinite
emotion, pulsing through the celestial ocean within, and
you harness this energy, without identification, and you
consciously direct it. You plunge deep into the abyss of
your own being in search of the pearl beyond all price,
and you discover it. You allow; you let go; you are
nonattached.

You are a Star. *You guide with ancient wisdom of the*
constellations. Shining at the crossroads, you illuminate the
way for those lost at sea seeking direction. You are brilliant,
dependable, and consistent. You have an inner compass;
you trust your intuitive guidance. Knowing your goal, you
establish clear standards and chart the course toward its
accomplishment. While glowing, you bestow good wishes to
all from the heavens. You sparkle and delight, even in the
dark of night.

The *balian's* energy shifted . . . I came out of trance. He chuckled. "I forgot number eight," he said. "That means I get to fill number eight with whatever I want," I replied with a smile. He burst out a big Buddha laugh.

The moment of silence following our conversation carried eternity with it. I looked at the *balian* and saw God in his eyes. Everywhere I looked I saw God. I smiled, holding my heart. I looked to the heavens and held my hands in prayer as a sign of gratitude for the story, with the Supreme revelation . . . I am the one who eternally navigates my vessel through the infinite sea with love, to any island of my heart's desire.

And so it is with you, Beloved. Therefore, prepare your boat, the *Astha-Brata* (Supreme Powers of Being), raise your sails, set your course, and launch. Put your heart, mind, and soul into the journey. Be the creator and the witness.

For me there is only the traveling on paths
that have heart, on any path that may have heart,
and the only worthwhile challenge is to
traverse its full length—and there I travel
looking, looking breathlessly.
—CARLOS CASTANEDA

SAILING IN SUPREME INFLUENCE

So . . . how does this story relate to Supreme Influence? The boat, the *Astha-Brata,* is your body temple, which you direct with your three sails. Your three sails—*idep* (pure thought), *sabda* (pure word), *bayu* (pure deed)—represent creative powers, which once harmonized toward a purposeful vision (your island) will unleash your Supreme Influence. *Idep* and *sabda* correspond with Logos, illuminating the power of thought and word to propel you toward your vision—how you consciously create as you speak. The infinite sea is your Supreme consciousness, which becomes calm as you become still. The sea transcends the cycles of birth, life, and death. It is the source from which all existence is created, sustained, and transformed. It is the omnipotent field from which *you*—the "I am"—speaks into existence. The helm represents the power of your will, steering you forward toward a worthy land. The island is your vision, or your inspirited goal. The compass is your discernment, informed by your feelings, which signals when you are on purpose or off course. The telescope is your "outcome frame," which allows you to focus on your ultimate destination. As you sail the infinite sea, you encounter crossroads, with limitless islands before you.

In the olden days there were pirates; it was a time when thieves set out to sea with the intent of exploring new lands, taking and conquering. They weren't *really* "thieves"; they were just sleepy travelers, without a *real* compass, unaware of who they are and why they live. In their delusion and distorted perceptions, they felt separate and hoarded to fill a void, which can only be filled through stillness and love. But this age is closing. The futility of it all has become clear. Even the pirates themselves are growing weary and beginning to see the pointlessness in taking that which will turn to dust.

At times in your life, you may have felt marooned on a deserted island without a map or strategy to chart a new course.

Perhaps the seas were turbulent, with violent winds giving rise to high tides, and you felt uncertain or scared to launch your voyage. Be still and have courage. Embracing the *new* means releasing the *old*. You must let go of old ways of thinking, speaking, and being to explore new territory, learn, grow, and evolve.

Whatever you can do, or dream you can,
begin it.
Boldness has genius, power, and magic in it.

—JOHANN WOLFGANG VON GOETHE

What if you are out at sea and your boat stops sailing? What if you go adrift or become lost? What if there is no wind behind your sails? What if your first mate or crew abandons ship? What keeps you sailing even in the midst of fog and storms? What inspires and sustains you to continue when you feel tired and weary? How do you balance the boat in turbulent waters? How do you ensure your sails are set true and leading you toward lands that will evoke the highest within you? How will you know which way to go when choice is before you? How will you discern when a new vision calls you, and it's time to move on? How will you let go when the time comes to embark on a new voyage?

The answer is simple. Love. Real love.

Love is the Source of energy fueling your boat, the *Astha-Brata* (Supreme Powers of Being). Love is the basis of our existence. Love fuels the natural forces of the universe—the sun, the moon, the earth, the wind, the fire, the water, and the stars. Love is the ultimate because love gives and receives all, without reservation, and requires nothing because it is whole and complete. Love praises, seeing the divine spark hidden within the heart of everyone. Love looks for what is good and what is right. Love is the expression of the truth within you. Love is who you are. Love is Supreme.

With love, conceive your vision in your mind's eye. Allow love to align your sails—*idep* (pure thought), *sabda* (pure word), and *bayu* (pure deed)—with your true purpose. Love creates inward fluency. With love, choose your words wisely, declare them with authority, ask purposeful questions, practice mantra, and wield the formulas you have learned to chart your course and guide yourself to the fulfillment of your ultimate destiny. Open your heart and use your telescope to look through "frames" that inspire and empower you to navigate the infinite sea regardless of circumstance toward the land of your highest calling. Be alert and listen to your intuitive guidance. You will know when it is time to set sail and when to come ashore.

You may choose to dock your boat, stay on land, build a sanctuary, and welcome other travelers. Or you may feel called to another land and set sail, embarking once again on a new voyage filled with awe and fresh possibility. Explore. Look out onto the horizon; grab hold of your telescope. Be still. Observe your compass, which points in the direction of your true purpose, guided by the voice of your intuition. When the time comes, prepare your boat and set sail. Do not hesitate; do not stumble or look back.

The sea contains all possibility. Within it there is dark and light, pleasure and pain, victory and defeat. However, you are not swayed by appearances. Instead you watch *what is*, the sea conditions, the weather, without attachment—for you understand all is eternally changing in the sea of infinite love.

Therefore, find certainty in the midst of uncertainty. Focus on your goal and navigate the sea. Allow the water to deepen you. Do not lose your *self* in the ever-changing swells. Be still. You will calm the sea by calming your mind.

If you collide with a *"Titanic"* along the way, experiencing miscommunication with another, know that beyond the challenge is a gift. There is a higher place where your spirits dwell and harmonize. You have all the resources to effectively commune, understand, transform challenges, bridge worlds, and throw a boat party.

Supreme Influence is at hand. This is a time where conscious beings, like you and me, navigate the infinite sea bestowing divine love and Supreme light. This is the journey before us, a journey of healing, a journey of awakening . . . our journey home.

Beloved, now is time to chart your voyage and embark on the Supreme adventure of *your* lifetime. Along your voyage you will encounter many others also sailing the infinite sea. Some you will simply pass with a wave, a smile, and a blessing. Others you will feel drawn toward, almost magnetically, as though you are destined to journey together, for a while. And so you do. Together with your beloveds, you sail until you arrive on the island of your shared vision. You disembark, ready to explore, and share your love with this new land and its people. You are here to give, not to take. You are here to enjoy and share in life's wonder. You came to offer the fullness of your gifts and contribute to elevating this new home, which you have chosen, for a while. Through your presence you breathe new life into this island. Through you it takes on new dimensions, awaking in the reflection of your present love. And so you embrace it, and it embraces you. You see yourself in the mirror of existence.

Everything in this land flourishes in the magic of your sacred affection. Everywhere you go, you are home, because you bring home with you. Your heart is your home, your love is your home, and when you share it, we are all home.

This is the journey of awakening . . . this is living in Supreme Influence.

The beginning.

Acknowledgments

With love in my heart, I wish to thank each person who has entered my life, those who touched, inspired, and illumined me through their presence.

I wish to acknowledge and express my deepest gratitude for Linda Ferrari, my soul sister and QOO (Queen of Operations). Your beautiful heart, brilliant mind, steadfast presence, and exquisite taste inspire my life's work. I am honored to share this grand vision with you. Thank you for being by my side.

My magnificent students, and most especially the mighty Light Workers who are Supreme Influence in Action (SIIA) graduates—you, each one of you, is the source of my deepest inspiration. It is my joy to join you in accomplishing the Great Work.

My amazing crew and volunteers, with deep gratitude I salute you. Thank you for so graciously and consistently showing up.

To my Beloved soul kin: My friend Ash, thank you for your insightful reflections, generous spirit, and hearty laughs. To

Nick Delgado, my friend, world champion, and health master, for being there. To Taylor Ferrari, for your intelligent observations. To Larisa Stow, I cherish our transcendental friendship and your sacred music. To Adil Panton, thank you for your unwavering support and for living the Lotus Sutra. To Demian Lichtenstein, for your heart and vision, you are a gift. To Shapoor Farahmand, the Lion, thank you for being the one I can count on 100 percent of the time. To Tzatzi Murphy and Andy Zubia, you are my earth angels. To Dawn Brown, thank you for your reflection and divine alignments. To Judson Neil, thank you for journeying with me through many realms. To Doc, I am grateful for our profound conversations that reveal new understandings to ancient wisdom. 93. Beloved Merrill, your magick reveals the gates of I AM. The veil is rent! And I stand awake and grateful for our divine connection in the Great Mystery. To Michael Shubert, thank you for your steadfast presence and genuine heart and for supporting me on many levels. I treasure you. To Michael Bernard Beckwith and the resplendent Agape community, and to those above, you are my soul family and I adore you with all my heart.

To those who contributed to this book: my editor Gary Jansen, thank you for being a great ally and challenger; your luminous reflection was priceless in delivering this work in its present form. To Kathy Klingaman, thank you for elegantly translating the images in my mind into manifest reality. To Barry Selby, thank you for capturing the moments. Gary Sweet and Paula Brisco, I appreciate your excellent copyediting.

To the pioneers who shared their knowledge and whom I have been blessed to learn from, I honor you, especially: Napoleon Hill, Tony Robbins, Richard Bandler, Master Choa Kok Sui, Master Co, and Deepak Chopra.

To the amazing leaders Garth Blumenthal, Chris Pass, and Stuart Johnson for opening doors of opportunity in the early days of my career.

To the one's who made a difference in my life early on, and who inspired my path, especially: Jim Rohn, Dr. Bredenburg, Anthony Fiorenza, and Fred Warren.

To my family of birth: Maria Teresa Hernandez, the most remarkable, most giving and strongest-willed woman I know, my mother, Mami. To the sweetest, most faithful man I know, my father, Valentin Hernandez, Papi. Thank you for being my gateway into this human adventure. To my brother Aaron, I love you. To Ayo, thank you for your kind spirit and our precious walks; and Aya, for taking care of me in my early years.

To the great avatars and enlightened masters whose lives modeled Supreme Influence incarnate, and to the scribes whose writings illuminated the way; I feel utmost reverence and thanksgiving for the wisdom you revealed—I Am That I Am.

About the Author

Niurka is a communication expert and transformational leader who inspires and empowers people to live genuinely, freely, and mightily. Her unique blend of linguistics, cognitive neuroscience, business, and spirituality guides people to transcend challenges, enrich relationships, and realize greater success in every area of life.

A former top corporate trainer for Anthony Robbins, Niurka launched her own training and consulting company in 2000, offering courses, seminars, and retreats that notably improve communication skills and transform lives. Her work has led tens of thousands of people to elevate the way they think, speak, and ultimately live.

Niurka is a master trainer of neuro-linguistic programming (NLP) and a master hypnotist, and her company is an accredited institute of NLP and hypnosis, offering global certification in these disciplines. She is a practitioner of Time Line Therapy and Pranic Healing as well as a business consultant, community builder, and mystic.

For further information, please contact Niurka's office at:
(866) 656–1001
www.NiurkaInc.com
info@NiurkaInc.com